BOB WILSON'S
SOCCER
QUIZ BOOK

—

Bob Wilson

with
William Walker

WILLOW BOOKS
Collins
8 Grafton Street, London, W1
1989

Willow Books
William Collins Sons & Co Ltd
London · Glasgow · Sydney · Auckland
Toronto · Johannesburg

First published 1989
© Bob Wilson and William Walker 1989

A CIP catalogue record for this book is
available from the British Library

ISBN 0 00 218356 0

Set in Palatino by Fox Lane Graphics, London
Printed and bound in Great Britain by
William Collins Sons & Co Ltd, Glasgow

INTRODUCTION

The great game of football never ceases to provide memorable moments along with incidents of controversy, oddity and amusement. There's no doubt also that a knowledge of soccer's history adds to its enjoyment.

Many fans pride themselves on being able to recall great goals and matches of the past as well as being 'clued up' on the present. I'm sure most of you have spent time on the terraces, at home or in your school, pub or club in friendly arguments about who won what, who plays where, who scored when or whatever. Now's your chance to have fun while testing your knowledge of the world's favourite sport.

To keep you amused, my colleague William Walker and I have compiled 3000 questions - ranging from Brechin to Barcelona and from Matthews to Maradona. Many of the questions are on recent seasons, although there are also quite a few on famous names and events of yesteryear.

Every aspect of soccer is covered - from the traditional posers on cups, leagues and players to more specialised ones on grounds, nicknames and unusual happenings. There are even some real 'trivia' questions on sponsors, celebrity supporters and football songs. Basically, if a football fan might know the answer then the question is asked. Captains and coaches, transfers and trophies, referees and rules - they are all in there somewhere!

Before you kick off, a word about how you might like to use the book. The 3000 questions are arranged in 500 quizzes of six questions each with the answers all at the back. The questions in each quiz come from six broad categories. These are:

1. BRITISH FOOTBALL
2. PLAYERS
3. EUROPEAN FOOTBALL
4. INTERNATIONAL FOOTBALL
5. SOCCER TRIVIA
6. GENERAL (A Mixed Bag)

All question no.1's are on British Football, all no. 2's on players etc. Therefore, players can answer either on a general 'as-they-come' basis or in a 'specialist subject' format. For example, if you think you're well-versed on international soccer, you could choose to answer a batch of question no. 4's. Remember that some are easy and some are real 'stinkers'! You can either quiz yourself or take on your family and friends. So get cracking and have fun!

Bob Wilson

QUIZ 1

1. Who played 663 League matches for West Ham between 1967 and 1987?
2. Name the former England international striker who celebrated his European Cup debut by heading the winner in the 1979 Final.
3. In which Dutch town is the professional football team of the Philips Sport Verein based?
4. Who captained England to World Cup glory in 1966?
5. What are the colours of Oxford United?
6. What is the height of a football goal?

QUIZ 2

1. Who scored the sensational injury-time goal which clinched the 1989 League Championship for Arsenal?
2. Who was West Ham's Bermudian striker of the late 1960s and early 70s?
3. Which European trophy was first contested in 1960-61?
4. Who was top goalscorer in the 1978 World Cup in Argentina?
5. Which team plays at The Dell?
6. Which England manager resigned his position for a lucrative job in the United Arab Emirates?

QUIZ 3

1. Name the Rangers midfielder who hit St Mirren's winner in the 1987 Scottish Cup Final.
2. Which two cousins teamed up at Spurs in 1985?
3. Which was the first British team to compete in the European Cup?
4. Who scored the first goal of England's qualifying campaign for the 1990 World Cup when he netted after 16 minutes of the away match in Albania?
5. What is the name of Sunderland's ground?
6. Other than Liverpool, which British club has played in the finals of all three European competitions?

QUIZ 4

1. Who is Arsenal's most capped player of all time?
2. Who is the striker, nicknamed 'Rambo', who notched 22 goals for Aston Villa during 1988-89?
3. The first European Cup was won by which famous club?
4. In the 1986 World Cup, who took over as England captain in the absence of Robson and Wilkins?
5. What is the most famous anthem of Liverpool's Kop choir?
6. In 1967, what was generally considered to have been the reason for Football League gates being up $1\frac{1}{2}$ million on the previous season?

QUIZ 5

1. Which Celtic and Scotland star was ordered off for a foul on Gordon Strachan in the 1984 Scottish Cup Final?
2. Name four of the five League clubs for which Peter Shilton has played from 1966 to 1989.
3. Which top European club is named after a legendary Greek hero?
4. Name the defender included in both Scotland's 1974 and 1978 World Cup squads without playing a match in either series.
5. Whose autobiography was entitled *Spurred to Success*?
6. Which Englishman became FIFA president in 1961?

QUIZ 6

1. Which club was once known as Singers FC?
2. Which Football League club brought top Danish striker Allan Simonsen to England in 1982?
3. West Ham were beaten 4-2 in the 1976 European Cup-Winners Cup Final by which Belgian team?
4. In which Mexican city did England play their 1986 World Cup group matches?
5. What was the title of the BBC programme which featured a general knowledge quiz between soccer teams?
6. Which Somerset-based non-League side is famous for its sloping pitch?

----------- **QUIZ 7** -----------

1. Who was the Aston Villa manager who led them to European Cup victory in 1982?
2. Who captained Dundee United to the Scottish and UEFA Cup Finals in 1987?
3. Who were the 1989 UEFA Cup winners?
4. Which international team was managed in the 1970s by Englishman Mike Smith?
5. Who is the top Irish international nicknamed 'Chippy'?
6. In 1949, which Italian club lost its entire team in a plane crash at Superga?

----------- **QUIZ 8** -----------

1. Who twice equalized for Everton in the 1989 FA Cup Final?
2. In 1979, whom did Liverpool sign from Maccabi Tel Aviv for £200,000?
3. Which team won the European Cup-Winners Cup for a record third time in 1989?
4. Who was manager of England's 1966 World Cup-winning team?
5. Who are 'The Gunners'?
6. England striker Gary Lineker collected his first winners medal in which tournament?

----------- **QUIZ 9** -----------

1. Which competition began in English Football in 1960?
2. Who was the Chelsea forward of the 1970s who became one of the first long-throw specialists?
3. Whose goal in the penalty shoot-out clinched the 1984 European Cup Final for Liverpool against Roma?
4. When West Germany won the World Cup in 1974, which country defeated them in a group match?
5. Which Welsh club plays at the Vetch Field?
6. Name the two Scottish clubs called 'Rovers'.

QUIZ 10

1. Who won the 1989 Scottish Cup?
2. Which Spurs player joined Arsenal in 1977 after thirteen years at White Hart Lane?
3. French star Just Fontaine played for which club in the 1959 European Cup Final?
4. Name the two England stars who both made their final international appearance as late substitutes in the 1982 World Cup match against Spain.
5. Singer David Essex is a fan of which London club?
6. How many players comprise a World Cup squad?

QUIZ 11

1. Which club reached the League Cup Final and won promotion to the First Division in 1975?
2. Who was the Norwegian goalkeeper signed by Spurs from Gothenburg for £450,000 in December 1988?
3. In which European country is the top division known as 'The Supreme League'?
4. Who scored England's first goal in the 1966 World Cup Tournament?
5. Which England star joined Henry Cooper in his admiration of 'The Great Smell of Brut'?
6. Which team changes if there is a clash of colours in a Football League match?

QUIZ 12

1. How many different clubs have won the Scottish Premier Division Championship?
2. David Cross was the Second Division's highest scorer in 1980-81. Which club was he then with?
3. Who was the Hungarian Real Madrid star who hit four goals in the 1960 European Cup Final?
4. Who scored Scotland's only goal of the 1986 World Cup Finals?
5. What feature is common to the grounds of Oldham, Preston and Luton Town?
6. In which month is the FA Cup Final usually played?

QUIZ 13

1. Where did England's World Cup winning boss Sir Alf Ramsey make a brief return to club management in 1977-78?
2. From which club did Chelsea sign Kerry Dixon in 1983?
3. What are the colours of the Swedish team IFK Gothenburg?
4. Name the striker, then with Newcastle United, who scored five goals for England against Cyprus in 1975.
5. In which part of Merseyside do Tranmere Rovers play?
6. Who was Watford manager for ten years before leaving for Aston Villa in May 1987?

QUIZ 14

1. With which club did Alf Ramsey win a League Championship medal as a player?
2. In which year did Liverpool sign Kenny Dalglish to replace Kevin Keegan?
3. What was the score in every European Cup Final from 1978 to 1983?
4. Which country eliminated Scotland from the 1974 World Cup Tournament after holding them to a 1-1 draw?
5. What is Watford's ground called?
6. Who succeeded Bobby Charlton as Footballer of the Year in 1967?

QUIZ 15

1. Which Midlands club lost in all four of its post-war FA Cup Final appearances?
2. Who was the striker bought by Middlesbrough from Manchester United for £700,000 during 1988-89?
3. Which Scottish club reached the European Cup semi-finals in 1963?
4. Who is the only player ever to score a hat-trick in a World Cup Final?
5. In 1987, which First Division club employed sports psychologist John Syer to help players identify strengths and weaknesses?
6. What is the maximum width of a football pitch?

QUIZ 16

1. In 1985, which club missed out on its first venture into European competition because of the UEFA ban on English sides?
2. From which club did Rangers sign Ray Wilkins in November 1987?
3. Which Hungarian side eliminated Manchester United in reaching the 1985 UEFA Cup Final?
4. What was the score in England's first meeting with Ireland in 1882?
5. In the comic *Tiger*, which club was run by Football Family Robinson?
6. Who won the 1986 Screen Sport Super Cup, beating Everton in the final?

QUIZ 17

1. Jimmy Armfield made 568 League appearances for which club?
2. Which 'Gerry' is the odd one out - Daly, Peyton, Armstrong or Ryan?
3. Helenio Herrera managed which club to European Cup success in the 1960s?
4. Who were the 1974 World Cup side known as 'The Leopards'?
5. Soviet Union goalkeeper Renat Dasayev is married to which famous Olympic gymnast?
6. At what distance from the goal is a penalty kick taken?

QUIZ 18

1. Bobby Stokes' goal won the FA Cup for which team in the 1970s?
2. With which club did goalkeeper Mervyn Day win a FA Cup-winners medal as a teenager?
3. Who was the substitute who headed Aberdeen's winner in their 1983 European Cup-Winners Cup triumph over Real Madrid?
4. In which year did Gary Lineker make his England debut, as a substitute against Scotland at Hampden?
5. What is the full name of Scottish First Division club Airdrie?
6. Alan Ball's first Football League managerial post was at which club?

QUIZ 19

1. Who was 'Shanks'?
2. With which team did striker John Deehan win a League Cup-winners medal in 1977?
3. In 1966, which Belgrade club became the first Eastern-bloc side to reach the European Cup Final?
4. In the 1986 World Cup, two countries lost all three of their matches - name either.
5. Who is the comedian who summed up supporting Birmingham City with the phrase 'You lose some, you draw some'?
6. Which company presented the 'Manager of the Month' awards for twenty years between 1969 and 1988?

QUIZ 20

1. Which was the last trophy won by Blackpool?
2. When Billy McNeill played for Celtic against Rangers in the 1969 Scottish Cup Final, which other top manager did he directly oppose?
3. Before 1972, by what name was the UEFA Cup competition known?
4. Name the Ipswich player who scored in six consecutive appearances for England during 1981-82.
5. Which team are known as 'The Belfast Blues'?
6. Which 'Town' became a 'City' in February 1970?

QUIZ 21

1. Nat Lofthouse won 33 caps for England while playing at which club?
2. John Aldridge is an international for which country?
3. Now in charge of the club's pools, who was the striker who hit Celtic's European Cup-winning goal in 1967?
4. In February 1989, which defender netted twice for Scotland during the World Cup match in Cyprus?
5. Which First Division team plays at Plough Lane?
6. How many substitutes sit on the bench in European and International matches?

QUIZ 22

1. Which First Division club was involved in a football betting and bribery scandal in 1963?
2. For which London side did stylish England midfielder Trevor Brooking play?
3. Where did Manchester United win the European Cup?
4. Which South American star of the 1970s was nicknamed 'The White Pele'?
5. Which unusual colour of goalkeeping jersey did Peter Shilton like to wear during his time at Leicester?
6. Who was the great football administrator and chairman of Burnley who died in 1981?

QUIZ 23

1. To which club did Manchester United pay £195,000 to acquire striker Ted MacDougall in 1972?
2. Which England midfielder was known as 'The Ghost' for the way he 'appeared' in goal-scoring positions?
3. For whom did AC Milan pay £5.5 million to PSV Eindhoven in 1987?
4. Which country did Glenn Hysen lead to a creditable 0-0 Wembley draw in England's opening World Cup qualifier of October 1988?
5. What is the nickname of Manchester United?
6. Which international manager was sacked as boss of Mansfield in 1979?

QUIZ 24

1. Whom did Graeme Souness succeed as Rangers manager in 1986?
2. In 1979, which Wolves player joined Manchester City for £1.4 million?
3. In November 1988, the planned demolition of which infamous European stadium was announced?
4. Name the defender who was the only Liverpool player to go to Mexico with England in 1970.
5. Who is the Danish international striker nicknamed 'The Bison'?
6. Which Everton star was voted Footballer of the Year in 1985-86?

QUIZ 25

1. Glaswegian Jimmy Sirrel was a long-serving manager at which club?
2. Since leaving Leeds in 1983, Terry Connor has starred for two clubs on the South Coast - can you name them?
3. In 1968-69, which British city had two teams in the European Cup?
4. Who was the Celtic full-back who played for Scotland in the 1974 and 1982 World Cups but missed out in 1978 through injury?
5. Which Scottish manager watches his team from an office overlooking the pitch?
6. Which colour of card does a referee show to indicate that he has sent off a player?

QUIZ 26

1. Who scored two extra-time goals to win the 1989 FA Cup for Liverpool?
2. Alan Devonshire is a full international for which country?
3. Which British side progressed furthest in European competition during 1988-89?
4. Giant striker Torres was a World Cup star for which country in 1966?
5. In the 1982 World Cup, which country had a mascot called 'Yer Man'?
6. Where was Howard Kendall's first managerial appointment?

QUIZ 27

1. Has Brentford ever played in Division One?
2. Which member of Ipswich's 1978 Cup Final team was forced to retire prematurely, leaving Britain to play part-time in Norway?
3. Which Italian club defeated both Celtic and Manchester United on its way to winning the 1969 European Cup?
4. Who scored the fastest-ever goal in the World Cup Finals, during the 1982 tournament?
5. Which newspaper sponsored the Football League?
6. In June 1989, former Leeds boss Billy Bremner began his second spell as manager of which other Yorkshire club?

QUIZ 28

1. Which club was formerly known as Bristol South End?
2. Name the midfielder who played under Brian Clough at Hartlepool, Derby, Leeds and Forest.
3. What does the acronym UEFA stand for?
4. Which top star was surprisingly dropped for Scotland's crucial match with Uruguay in the 1986 World Cup?
5. What is the surname of 'Roy of the Rovers'?
6. Which Lancashire seaside town has been the traditional headquarters of the Football League?

QUIZ 29

1. Who replaced Lawrie McMenemy as manager at Southampton in 1985?
2. Who scored five goals for Middlesbrough in their 9-0 thrashing of Brighton in 1958?
3. The highest-ever European Cup crowd saw Celtic beat which English club at Hampden in 1970?
4. Trevor Francis was first capped at which club?
5. What is the club song of West Ham?
6. Which was Trevor Francis' North American Soccer League club?

QUIZ 30

1. Before Arsenal in 1989, which was the last team from outside of Merseyside to win the First Division?
2. Scottish World Cup full-back Willie Donachie, recently a player-coach at Oldham, appeared in over 350 First Division games for which club?
3. To which Dutch club did Celtic lose the 1970 European Cup Final?
4. In the 1978 World Cup, which country's goalkeeper was booked for fouling a Polish player in the Polish half of the field?
5. What number did Gary Lineker wear during the 1986 World Cup?
6. Inverness Clachnacuddin and Forres Mechanics play in which league?

QUIZ 31

1. Which player, recently with Ipswich Town, scored the winner for Rangers against Dundee United in the the 1981 Scottish League Cup Final?
2. At which club did Derby striker Paul Goddard begin his goalscoring career?
3. Which Greek club did Ferenc Puskas guide to the 1971 European Cup Final at Wembley?
4. Who was the Derby player who missed a penalty in Scotland's opening World Cup match of 1978?
5. What is the name of Tottenham Hotspur's ground?
6. Which club did manager David Pleat serve for eight years before leaving to join Tottenham in May 1986?

QUIZ 32

1. Goalkeeper Sam Bartram was a star of yesteryear - for which club did he play?
2. Which international midfielder joined Rangers from Everton in June 1989?
3. What is the name of the top Czechoslovakian army team?
4. Name the manager who led Belgium in successful European Championship and World Cup campaigns during the 1980s.
5. What is Diego Maradona's middle name?
6. Name one of the clubs for which Diego Maradona played before joining Napoli.

QUIZ 33

1. With which club did full-back Geoff Palmer play in two League Cup winning sides?
2. Which Chelsea striker bagged five goals in the away match at Walsali in February 1989?
3. Which German team beat Inter-Milan 7-1 in 1971, only to be ordered to replay because of missile-throwing?
4. Who is England's top international goalscorer of all time?
5. At which Scottish ground might you stand in 'The Jungle'?
6. In 1970, a new British Cup competition was started - by what name was it known?

QUIZ 34

1. Which World Cup hero of 1966 had a spell as manager of Chelsea from 1979 to 1981?
2. What is the name of David O'Leary's brother who won a Scottish Cup medal with Celtic in 1985?
3. Which Dutch club won three consecutive European Cups from 1971 to 1973?
4. In the 1970 World Cup, from whose header did Gordon Banks make one of the most famous saves of all time?
5. With which top striker was TV personality Suzanne Dando once romantically linked?
6. What is Pele's full name?

QUIZ 35

1. Who made 655 League appearances for Chelsea as well as leading them to victory in the 1970 FA Cup Final?
2. From which club did Hearts sign John Colquhoun in 1985?
3. Which Spanish club had three players sent off in a 1974 European Cup tie against Celtic at Parkhead?
4. Which former star player took over management of the French national side in November 1988?
5. What is the profession of Mexican World Cup star Hugo Sanchez?
6. Who usually compete for the FA Charity Shield?

QUIZ 36

1. Which club was once known as Ardwick FC?
2. Former England skipper Gerry Francis won all of his twelve international caps with which club?
3. Which team won the one and only replayed European Cup Final in 1974 - the first of three consecutive successes?
4. Name the current League manager who made one appearance for England in the 1970 World Cup, scoring from a penalty against Czechoslovakia.
5. D.J. Andy Peebles supports which of the Manchester teams?
6. Pat Partridge performed which footballing role?

QUIZ 37

1. Which Third Division club defeated Glasgow Rangers on its way to winning the 1980-81 Anglo-Scottish Cup?
2. For which club did defender Micky Droy play from 1971 to 1985?
3. Which Scottish striker opened the scoring for Everton in their 1985 European Cup-Winners Cup Final against Rapid Vienna?
4. Which country was unbeaten in the 1978 World Cup but still finished only third?
5. Why did Morocco's Mohammed Timouni probably have the dirtiest boots in the 1986 World Cup?
6. What was the name of Chicago's North American Soccer League Team?

QUIZ 38

1. In what way were the FA Cup Finals of 1981, 1982 and 1983 similar?
2. Whom did Neville Southall replace as Wales' regular goalkeeper?
3. Which manager took Leeds to the European Cup Final in 1975?
4. Who was playing on his home ground, when he scored to clinch Scotland's place in the 1978 World Cup, in the away qualifying match against Wales?
5. What does Everton goalkeeper Neville Southall collect for a hobby - clocks, stamps or garden gnomes?
6. During a penalty shoot-out, where should non-participating players be?

QUIZ 39

1. Jimmy Hill was a successful manager with which Midlands side?
2. Which Ipswich striker scored five goals against Southampton in 1982?
3. Which club's fans shout 'Allez Les Verts'?
4. Who was the striker who opened the scoring for West Germany in the 1966 World Cup Final?
5. At which ground can you not use the car park on St Leger day?
6. What is the full name of Kidderminster's GM Vauxhall Conference side?

QUIZ 40

1. Jim Cannon played over 500 games for which club?
2. Which striker, then with Norwich City, was the Second Division's top scorer in 1985-86?
3. Who was the Derby County star who hit a hat-trick against Real Madrid in 1975?
4. Which country caused a sensation in the 1974 World Cup when Emmanuel Sanon shot them ahead against Italy?
5. What are the colours of Plymouth Argyle?
6. How many clubs are in the Football League?

QUIZ 41

1. Who is Derby County's most capped player?
2. Which player made his debut for Liverpool at Wembley, in the 1977 Charity Shield?
3. In which European country does Omonia Nicosia play?
4. What was the name of Holland's goalkeeper in the 1974 and 1978 World Cups?
5. Who is BBC Scotland's leading football commentator?
6. Which league did Barrow win in 1988-89?

QUIZ 42

1. John Carey once managed which of the Merseyside clubs?
2. Can you name the striker, born in French Guyana, who scored 82 League goals for West Bromwich before joining Coventry in 1984?
3. Where did Liverpool win their first European Cup in 1977?
4. Despite finishing second, which team, in most people's opinion, were considered to have been the best in the 1974 World Cup won by West Germany?
5. Who is the international manager who once presented a TV programme on country pursuits?
6. How many classifications of free-kick are there?

QUIZ 43

1. Johnny Haynes played for which London team?
2. Name the centre-half who, in 1982, won a European Cup medal with Aston Villa and played for Scotland in the World Cup Finals.
3. In which European city is the massive Nou Camp stadium?
4. As well as Scotland, which other Commonwealth country qualified for the 1974 World Cup?
5. What was the name of England's lion mascot in the 1966 World Cup?
6. Who was the Liverpool full-back who scored vital goals during normal time in two European Cup Finals?

QUIZ 44

1. From which other London club did Fulham sign Peter Kitchen for £150,000 in 1979?
2. Who was Liverpool's 'Super-sub' of the late 1970s?
3. Liverpool's first goal against Moenchengladbach in the 1977 European Cup Final was scored by which midfielder?
4. Who scored Northern Ireland's goal in their famous 1982 World Cup victory over hosts Spain?
5. Where do Ipswich Town play?
6. Which former England captain played for Team America against England in the US Bicentennial game of 1976?

QUIZ 45

1. Who was the Fulham star transferred to Liverpool for £333,333 in 1980?
2. Striker Wayne Clarke began his career with which club?
3. Ernst Happel took which Belgian team to the 1978 European Cup Final against Liverpool at Wembley?
4. What was the score in every opening match of the World Cup Finals from 1966 to 1978?
5. Which member of the Royle family has played football at Wembley?
6. What number did Manchester City goalkeeper Len Langford wear in the 1933 FA Cup Final?

QUIZ 46

1. With which team did Irving Nattrass appear at Wembley in the 1976 League Cup Final?
2. Which club did Trevor Francis leave to go to Italy in 1982?
3. In 1968, Leeds defeated which Hungarian side to take the Fairs Cup?
4. In which Spanish city is the San Mames stadium where England played their 1982 World Cup group matches?
5. Which Scottish team plays in red and white hooped jerseys?
6. Whom did Graham Kelly replace as Secretary of the Football Association?

QUIZ 47

1. Brian Clough once managed which North-Eastern club?
2. At which club did Mark Falco begin his career?
3. Which is the smallest town from which a European Cup winning team has come?
4. Rangers striker Colin Stein scored four goals for Scotland in a 1969 World Cup qualifier - against which small island country?
5. Which soccer personality's autobiography was entitled *This One's on Me*?
6. In a penalty shoot-out, what is the minimum number of kicks a team must take before it can win?

QUIZ 48

1. In which year was Hereford United elected to the Football League?
2. Which current top striker is known as 'Fash'?
3. Antonin Panenka starred in midfield for which European national side?
4. Which country came from 2-0 down to knock holders England out of the 1970 World Cup?
5. What is the name of the Rugby League ground where Bradford City played many home games after the Valley Parade fire of 1985?
6. The Scottish League was first sponsored by which company?

QUIZ 49

1. Ex-Arsenal player and manager Terry Neill played also for which Humberside club?
2. Who was the blond-haired striker who netted 18 goals in Aston Villa's championship season of 1980-81?
3. Which Scandanavian team did Forest defeat in Munich to win their first European Cup in 1979?
4. Who was the famous striker who made his final international appearance for Scotland in the 1974 World Cup match with Zaire?
5. In which town did Jack play for United and Jimmy for City, according to *Scorcher*?
6. Can a football pitch be square?

QUIZ 50

1. Who captained Aberdeen to three straight Scottish Cup wins from 1982 to 1984?
2. Name the former Leicester captain who, in May 1987, made his Scotland debut at the age of 29 and four months later, signed for Everton in a £300,000 deal.
3. Who was the English manager who took Malmo of Sweden to the 1979 European Cup Final?
4. Wales faced which two powerful national sides in their qualifying matches for the 1990 World Cup?
5. What is the football fans' version of the John Lennon song 'Give Peace a Chance'?
6. Peter Swales has been the long-serving chairman of which club?

QUIZ 51

1. Which Football League club did the late Jock Stein manage for 44 days in 1978?
2. With which club did Paul Allen begin his League career?
3. Which Italian club were the first winners of the European Cup-Winners Cup?
4. Where was the 1970 World Cup held?
5. Who is the former Liverpool skipper who also captained one of the teams in BBC's 'A Question of Sport'?
6. What was the name of the Los Angeles team for which George Best played?

QUIZ 52

1. What is Leeds United's record victory - set up against Lyn Oslo in the 1969-70 European Cup?
2. Everton's 1989 Cup Final skipper Kevin Ratcliffe plays international football for which country?
3. Which English star played against Nottingham Forest in the 1980 European Cup Final?
4. Who captained Scotland in the 1974 World Cup Finals?
5. Describe the style of jersey worn by Blackburn Rovers?
6. In which season was Kevin Keegan voted Footballer of the Year?

QUIZ 53

1. Which Scot is Leeds United's top goalscorer of all-time?
2. Who was the Aston Villa goalkeeper of the 1970s who also played cricket for Worcestershire?
3. What are the colours of Dynamo Kiev?
4. Who was the top goalscorer in the 1966 World Cup Tournament in England?
5. Which South Coast club are nicknamed 'The Seagulls'?
6. The Division Three record attendance of 49,309 was set up in 1979 - at a derby match in which city?

QUIZ 54

1. In 1987, which club won the first major trophy of its 104 year history?
2. Which player made over 100 appearances for each of Blackpool, Everton, Arsenal and Southampton?
3. Which Bulgarian club ended Forest's winning run in Europe by eliminating them from the Champions Cup in 1980-81?
4. Who was the England vice-captain who received his marching orders against Morocco in the 1986 World Cup?
5. Ashton Gate is home to which club?
6. Who became manager of the Republic of Ireland in 1986?

QUIZ 55

1. Whom did David Pleat replace as Leicester City boss in 1987?
2. Northern Ireland striker Colin Clarke scored a hat-trick on his First Division debut for which club in 1986?
3. Liverpool beat which Scottish club on a 5-0 aggregate on their way to winning the 1981 European Cup?
4. Name the Arsenal defender who made his England debut in 1987, in the 4-2 win over Spain in Madrid.
5. Which top British track athlete is a Sunderland fan?
6. What is the radius of the centre circle?

QUIZ 56

1. Ex-Derby striker Roger Davies returned from Bruges in 1977 to join which team?
2. Name the 5ft 4ins Welsh international who played for, amongst others, Burnley and Leeds.
3. In 1989, which club became Turkey's first-ever European Cup semi-finalists?
4. Tomas Boy was captain of which country during the 1986 World Cup?
5. Although a different colour, Hibernian's jersey is similar in style to which top English team's?
6. After leading Malmo to the European Cup Final, at which English club did Bob Houghton replace Alan Dicks as manager?

QUIZ 57

1. Who has won the most caps as a Liverpool player?
2. Former England cricket captain Mike Gatting has a brother who has played for Arsenal and Brighton - what's his name?
3. Which Spanish club did Liverpool defeat to lift the 1981 European Cup?
4. What colour was the change strip worn by Scotland from 1985 to 1988?
5. In which British city does Glentoran play?
6. What was the dramatic name of Kenya's only professional club, disbanded in February 1987 after being left out of a new Superleague?

QUIZ 58

1. Which player has made the most all-time appearances for Liverpool?
2. Former England striker Luther Blissett spent the 1983-84 season in Italy - with which club?
3. Who scored the vital equalizer for Spurs in their 1-1 draw in the 1984 UEFA Cup Final 2nd leg against Anderlecht?
4. For which country did Park Chang-Sun score with a screaming shot against Argentina in the 1986 World Cup?
5. *A Light in the North* was written by which top soccer manager?
6. Which is the only British club to have won both the European Cup-Winners Cup and the UEFA Cup?

QUIZ 59

1. When did Liverpool last play in Division Two?
2. For which club did former Wales striker Ron Davies score in ten consecutive appearances during the 1966-67 season?
3. Who scored Aston Villa's winner in their 1982 European Cup Final victory in Rotterdam?
4. What are the national colours of El Salvador?
5. What was called the 'Snatch of the Day' during the 1978-79 season?
6. May a player taking a penalty backheel the ball for a team-mate to shoot?

QUIZ 60

1. Striker Paul Mariner won FA Cup and UEFA Cup medals with which club?
2. Which First Division goalkeeper has been capped for Zimbabwe?
3. In which colour of shirts did Aston Villa win the European Cup in 1982?
4. Which country held reigning champions Italy to a 1-1 draw in the opening match of the 1986 World Cup in Mexico?
5. Who were the Spurs stars who had a hit single with 'Diamond Lights' in 1987?
6. Which was the first current League club to contest an FA Cup Final?

QUIZ 61

1. Who was 'Bill Nick' to the Tottenham players?
2. Name the full-back who is the only player to have won three FA Cup medals with Manchester United.
3. Which club has won the League of Ireland most often?
4. Which country did England defeat in the 1966 World Cup semi-finals?
5. If you travelled down Gorgie Road in Edinburgh, which team would you be going to see?
6. Which Canadian city has a team called 'Blizzard'?

QUIZ 62

1. Alan Oakes played 565 League matches for which club between 1959 and 1976?
2. Who was the Welsh international forward hailed in 1980 as 'The New Kevin Keegan'?
3. For how many consecutive years did English teams win the European Cup from 1977 inclusive?
4. Which European country did the Soviet Union thrash 6-0 in the 1986 World Cup?
5. What was the title of the film in which Pele and Bobby Moore played prisoners-of-war?
6. Who was the first professional player to be sent off at Wembley?

QUIZ 63

1. Which team did the League and FA Cup 'Double' in 1960-61?
2. For which Scottish club did George Best play?
3. Who is the Polish international striker who moved from Juventus to Roma in 1985?
4. Who was the England centre-forward nicknamed the 'Lion of Vienna' after a magnificent display against Austria in 1952?
5. What is the traditional shirt colour of Barnsley?
6. What did the Alliance Premier Division become in 1984?

QUIZ 64

1. Who managed Manchester United to European Cup glory in 1968?
2. Which Liverpool player skippered Falkirk at the age of 17?
3. Name the left-footed international midfielder who struck Hamburg's 1983 European Cup-winning goal.
4. Name Paraguay's 1985 South American Player of the Year who was a big hit in the World Cup of '86.
5. Dean Court is the home of which South Coast club?
6. Which First Division club has operated a controversial 'members only' policy in recent seasons?

QUIZ 65

1. Harry Hood was a prolific scorer with which club in the 1970s?
2. Which Manchester United defender won over 50 caps for Northern Ireland while playing with Luton?
3. Name the Seville-based club which plays in green and white striped jerseys.
4. Which Brazilian forward scored the goal which beat England in the famous World Cup match of 1970?
5. After whom was the original World Cup trophy named?
6. Why did the Football League advise champions Chelsea not to compete in the first-ever European Cup in 1955?

QUIZ 66

1. Newton Heath became which famous club?
2. Who played for Dundee United in the 1974 Scottish Cup Final and for Everton in the English version ten years later?
3. Which European tournament was won by Manchester City in 1970?
4. Who skippered Northern Ireland's team during the 1986 World Cup in Mexico?
5. The Sky Blue Stand can be found at which ground?
6. Name three Football League clubs called 'County'.

QUIZ 67

1. How many post-war seasons has Manchester United spent in Division Two?
2. Name the 1970s Test Match cricketer who played soccer for Huddersfield, Carlisle and Doncaster.
3. Who is the West German midfielder who joined Real Madrid in 1988 after eight years with arch-rivals Barcelona?
4. Who was England's youngest-ever captain, making his debut in 1962?
5. What was the title of the England World Cup Squad's chart-topping record of 1970?
6. Officially, how long is half-time, unless otherwise decided by the referee?

QUIZ 68

1. Wilf Mannion was a star in the 1940s and 50s with which club?
2. With which club did full-back John Gidman begin his soccer career?
3. Where did Liverpool beat Roma on penalties to lift the 1984 European Cup?
4. Which England player miscued the clearance from which Maradona scored his infamous first goal in the World Cup match of 1986?
5. For which part of the football media does Peter Jones work?
6. Who was the goalkeeper sent off three times while playing for Wrexham in 1982-83?

QUIZ 69

1. Striker Derek Possee scored 79 goals for which London side between 1967 and 1973?
2. What is the surname of brothers Mark and Brian who played together at Luton Town?
3. In which Italian city would you find the stadium known as San Siro?
4. Poland eliminated two British nations in the qualifying competition for the 1974 World Cup - which two?
5. In 1982, which team, according to Terry Venables, was 'setting English football back ten years'?
6. How many clubs play in the Third Round of the FA Cup?

QUIZ 70

1. Which former Manchester United star resigned as Burnley manager in 1985 after only 110 days in the job?
2. Name the Scottish international goalkeeper bought by Hibs from Oldham in October 1987.
3. Bjorn Nordqvist made 115 appearances for which European country between 1963 and 1978?
4. Name the midfielder, then with Anderlecht, who skippered Belgium's successful 1986 World Cup team.
5. Which First Division stadium is situated near to a Test Cricket ground of the same name?
6. Who was the Dutchman voted England's Footballer of the Year in 1981?

QUIZ 71

1. Elisha Scott was a famous goalkeeper at which club?
2. How many League games did Clive Allen play during his spell at Arsenal?
3. Which team beat Barcelona on penalties to win the 1986 European Cup?
4. For which country did Didier Six star in the 1978 and 1982 World Cups?
5. Which tobacco company has produced a comprehensive football yearbook since 1970?
6. What is the popular name of the rule which decides the winner of European ties, in the event of the teams' scores being level on aggregate?

QUIZ 72

1. Which club, placed third in Division Two in 1977, had by the following season, become First Division Champions?
2. Who is the former Dundee, Spurs and Scotland striker nicknamed 'Gillie'?
3. Which manager took Barcelona to the Spanish League Championship in 1985 and the European Cup Final one year later?
4. Besides Wembley, which London stadium was used for the 1966 World Cup?
5. What colour of shirts do Blackpool wear?
6. Which League club has been managed by Bill Dodgin senior, Bill Dodgin junior and Alec Stock?

QUIZ 73

1. Which Football League club renamed itself in 1987?
2. Who was the 1960s Rangers and Scotland wing-half known as 'Slim Jim'?
3. Which country k.o'd hosts Italy in reaching the Final of the 1980 European Championships where they lost 2-1 to West Germany?
4. Which Scotland manager of the 1970s played in the 1954 World Cup in Switzerland?
5. Where did Everton play immediately prior to moving to Goodison Park?
6. How did Tommy Lawton manage to score all of Everton's goals in the 1939-40 season?

QUIZ 74

1. At which club have both Bobby Moore and David Webb been manager during the 1980s?
2. For which country was John Mahoney capped?
3. Which is the only East German team to have won a European trophy - the 1974 Cup-Winners Cup?
4. What was the half-time score in the famous 1966 World Cup Final?
5. Which common feature is missing from the Celtic jersey?
6. For which English club did former Celtic boss Davie Hay play in the 1970s?

QUIZ 75

1. Name the ex-West Bromwich Albion defender who was in charge at Peterborough from 1983 to 1986.
2. Who was the Oxford and Northern Ireland striker forced to quit through injury in October 1986?
3. Which player did Aston Villa lose after only eight minutes of the 1982 European Cup Final?
4. Which country went to war with El Salvador after losing a World Cup qualifying match in 1969?
5. Name the First Division goalkeeper who plays in a brass band.
6. Who was the first non-English Footballer of the Year?

QUIZ 76

1. Which 'champagne and cigars' manager had two spells as boss of Plymouth Argyle?
2. At the end of the 1988-89 season, who was the longest-serving member of the Liverpool first team squad?
3. Which Scot captained Newcastle to European Fairs Cup success in 1969?
4. Who was the Coventry goalkeeper who travelled to Argentina with the Scotland World Cup squad in 1978?
5. Labour MP Roy Hattersley is a fan of which Yorkshire club?
6. What is Liverpool's lowest final League position in any of the last twenty seasons?

QUIZ 77

1. Has Birmingham City ever won the FA Cup?
2. Who is the big Newcastle-born centre-half who has played for Gillingham, Norwich and recently Manchester United?
3. Who were the 1989 Italian Champions?
4. Chivadze and Shengalia both scored for which country against Scotland in the 1982 World Cup?
5. At which London ground do away fans stand at the Clock End?
6. By what name was AFC Bournemouth known prior to 1971?

QUIZ 78

1. Jimmy Dickinson made 764 League appearances for which Southern club?
2. In 1986, Notts County player Rachid Harkouk appeared in the World Cup for which country?
3. Who wore the No.5 jersey in Celtic's European Cup Final win of 1967?
4. Which Spanish striker hit four goals to burst Denmark's bubble in the 1986 World Cup?
5. What, in football parlance, is 'Going over the top'?
6. Which non-League side has been managed by both Geoff Hurst and Gordon Banks?

QUIZ 79

1. In 1967, which was the first team to win the Football League Cup in a Wembley Final?
2. For which club did midfielder Ian Bowyer play over 400 matches?
3. Which great European star of the 1960s was born in Mozambique?
4. Which Scandanavian country held Wales to a 2-2 draw in the Swansea World Cup match of October 1988?
5. Which song is the 'Geordie National Anthem', sung by fans of Newcastle and Sunderland?
6. Why are no European competition matches played during January and February?

QUIZ 80

1. Which club did Bobby Charlton join as player-manager after leaving Manchester United?
2. With which club did winger Arthur Graham win all of his Scottish caps?
3. Which famous team did Celtic beat to take the European Cup in 1967?
4. Name the Soviet forward who hit a World Cup hat-trick against Belgium in 1986.
5. Why did 10,000 people turn up at Highfield Road in October 1965, while Coventry were playing in Cardiff?
6. What was the full name of Washington's NASL team?

QUIZ 81

1. Goalkeeper Steve Death played 471 League matches for which club from 1969 to 1982?
2. Which England star was nicknamed 'Hadleigh'?
3. Which German team stopped England's run of European Cup wins in the early 1980s?
4. Who was appointed Northern Ireland's player-manager in 1971?
5. Why did India withdraw from the 1950 World Cup?
6. For which country was Wigan boss Bryan Hamilton an international cap?

QUIZ 82

1. Emlyn Hughes was once player-manager of which Yorkshire team?
2. For which Midlands club has Bryan Robson's young brother Gary played since 1983?
3. Which country boasts the largest selection of European Cup-winning clubs?
4. Who celebrated his 41st birthday by winning a record 119th international cap during the 1986 World Cup Finals in Mexico?
5. Which Scottish team wears red and white, plays at Annfield Park and once had a manager named Shankly?
6. What was the approximate crowd at the Brazil-Uruguay World Cup match in the Maracana, Rio de Janeiro in 1950?

QUIZ 83

1. Argentinian Alex Sabella joined which League club in 1978?
2. With which club did Scottish international Richard Gough begin his career?
3. How many different Football League clubs have won a European Tournament - 9, 11 or 13?
4. Whom did Bobby Robson succeed as England Manager?
5. Which famous manager once said 'Football's not a matter of life and death - it's more important than that'?
6. Who was the veteran Hearts star named Scottish Footballer of the Year in 1986?

QUIZ 84

1. Which World Cup medallist had a spell as player-manager of Sheffield United?
2. From which neighbouring club did Birmingham sign Des Bremner in 1984?
3. Which was the last team to lift the European Cup playing in its own country?
4. Which Asian country caused a sensation in the 1966 World Cup by beating Italy 1-0 at Middlesbrough?
5. The Manor Ground is home to which club?
6. At which club did England boss Bobby Robson begin his playing career in 1950?

QUIZ 85

1. Name the Sheffield Wednesday goalkeeper who won 33 caps for England in the 1960s.
2. Which major Scottish club once turned down Kenny Dalglish after a trial?
3. Name the West German star who lost out to Liverpool in two European Cup Finals, with Moenchengladbach and with Real Madrid.
4. Which Blackburn Rovers full-back was the only Second Division player in England's 1970 World Cup squad?
5. Which football team had a chart hit record with 'Blue is the Colour' in 1972?
6. Who was the Irishman who resigned as Chelsea boss in 1979?

QUIZ 86

1. Terry Paine played most of his 824 League games for which club?
2. Which Second Division club signed Soviet internationalist Sergei Baltacha from Dynamo Kiev in 1988?
3. Which Englishman played against Liverpool in the 1981 European Cup Final in Paris?
4. Which country dumped holders Italy out of the 1986 World Cup?
5. Of which club was ITV commentator Brian Moore once a director?
6. By what name are Rangers and Celtic collectively known?

QUIZ 87

1. Which team lead the 1988-89 First Division at Christmas?
2. Which midfielder, later to join Derby, scored one goal and was voted 'Man of the Match' in Oxford's 1986 Milk Cup victory?
3. Which Nottingham Forest striker walked out on the club before the 1980 European Cup Final?
4. Who is Wales' most capped player?
5. In the 1974 World Cup, which competing team ate monkeys' heads as part of their training diet?
6. Who were 'The Three' who defeated 'The Six' 2-0 at Wembley in January 1973?

QUIZ 88

1. David Smallman was an international striker for which country during the 1970s?
2. Name the Guernsey-born winger who starred for Southampton during 1988-89.
3. Which Scottish club reached the UEFA Cup Final in 1987?
4. Other than Geoff Hurst, who scored for England in their World Cup Final victory?
5. Which Lancashire side plays in claret and sky blue?
6. Which player scored a hat-trick in the nostalgic rematch of the 1966 World Cup Final in aid of the Bradford disaster appeal?

QUIZ 89

1. John Trollope played over 700 League games for which club?
2. Tony Henry began his career at which of the Manchester clubs before moving on to Bolton, Oldham and Stoke?
3. Who were the first British winners of the European Cup?
4. Name the Arsenal and Wales goalkeeper who played for Britain against the Rest of Europe in 1955.
5. Which mythical creature is featured on Liverpool's badge?
6. Which is the only team to have won the 'Non-League Double' - the FA Trophy and Gola League?

QUIZ 90

1. Which member of the Arsenal 'Double'-winning side also played for QPR, Leicester, Notts County, Bournemouth and Torquay?
2. Tony Cascarino is an international for which country?
3. In 1980, who was the striker who scored for Forest against Barcelona in the European Super Cup during a brief spell at the City Ground?
4. Name the successful Argentinian manager in the 1986 World Cup.
5. Which Spurs defender was musically praised by the 'Cockerel Chorus' in 1973?
6. Which club did Denis Smith manage for five years, before taking over at Sunderland in May 1987?

QUIZ 91

1. Name the manager who led Spurs to FA Cup triumphs in 1981 and 1982.
2. Who was the Leeds and England forward known as 'Sniffer'?
3. Which Scottish team reached the first European Cup-Winners Cup Final?
4. Which former Football League striker notched the decisive goal in the exciting 1986 Belgium-USSR World Cup match?
5. What caused the abandonment of the Chester-Plymouth League Cup tie in September 1981?
6. In Glasgow's 'Old Firm' league matches, who has won more games - Celtic or Rangers?

QUIZ 92

1. Who is Tottenham's leading scorer of all time?
2. Goalkeeper Peter Hucker played in the 1982 FA Cup Final - for which team?
3. Which team plays in Madrid's Vicente Calderon Stadium?
4. Who was the Everton player who was first choice centre-half for England in the 1970 World Cup?
5. Which sportswear company introduced red and blue trims onto England's white shirt in 1974?
6. In the Laws of the Game, which of the following are compulsory - corner-flags, half-way flags or goal-nets?

QUIZ 93

1. Spurs' record defeat was in 1978 - who beat them 7-0?
2. From which club did Chelsea sign goalkeeper Dave Beasant in January 1989?
3. Why did Leicester compete in the 1961-62 Cup-Winners Cup despite losing in the 1961 FA Cup Final?
4. Which was the only country to remain undefeated in the 1974 World Cup Finals?
5. Which club plays at Home Park?
6. Who was the England star beaten-up by airport guards during a soccer trip to Yugoslavia in 1974?

—— QUIZ 94 ——

1. Which leading Scottish club celebrated its centenary in 1988?
2. When Glyn Hodges played for Wales in 1984, he became the first-ever international at which club?
3. Which was the first British team to win a European trophy?
4. Vasily Rats scored with a screaming shot against France in the 1986 World Cup - for which country does he play?
5. What was Sheffield Wednesday's change strip for the 1988-89 season?
6. What was the typically-American name given to the championship-deciding match in the North American Soccer League?

—— QUIZ 95 ——

1. Who is Watford's most-capped England player?
2. Who is the Welsh international winger who played in the First Division with Burnley, Derby, QPR, Swansea and Sunderland?
3. Which German team did West Ham defeat at Wembley to take the 1965 Cup-Winners Cup?
4. In winning the 1970 World Cup, which country did Brazil trounce 4-1 in the Final?
5. What was the title of Andy Cameron's 1978 hit record about the Scotland World Cup squad and its manager?
6. What is the full-name of the non-League side from Northwich?

—— QUIZ 96 ——

1. In which year did Spurs last win the League Championship?
2. Name the former Ipswich striker who scored 19 goals in Sunderland's Third Division Championship side of 1987-88.
3. Hammarby, 1985 UEFA Cup conquerors of St Mirren, play in which Swedish city?
4. Apart from winners Italy, there were two other unbeaten sides in the 1982 World Cup - name either of them.
5. Gresty Road is home to which club?
6. Before Arsenal's triumph in 1989, for how many consecutive seasons had the League Championship gone to Merseyside?

QUIZ 97

1. Which unenviable League record do Hartlepool hold?
2. Who was the Wimbledon goalkeeper who won fame in 1975 by saving a Peter Lorimer penalty in an FA Cup tie with Leeds?
3. In 1989, which club paid an estimated £4 million to secure the services of PSV defender Ronald Koeman?
4. Ex-Ipswich defender Allan Hunter was an international for which country?
5. Which BBC commentator once turned out for Stockport County reserves?
6. Who, in November 1988, became Britain's first-ever player/manager/director?

QUIZ 98

1. Which member of Manchester United's 1968 European Cup team left Old Trafford to join Middlesbrough for £20,000 in 1971?
2. Who was the full-back who moved from Blackburn to Leeds for £357,000 in 1979?
3. Who clipped a Graeme Souness pass into the net for Liverpool's winning goal in the 1978 European Cup Final at Wembley?
4. In April 1989, who scored his first goal for England with a great solo effort against Albania at Wembley?
5. What did Stranraer do without for the first 110 years of their history?
6. Which competition became the Freight Rover Trophy in 1984-85?

QUIZ 99

1. England star Billy Wright played for which club?
2. Which former QPR and England full-back joined Aldershot as player-coach in 1982?
3. Name the Czech team from Bratislava which eliminated Dunfermline at the semi-final stage in winning the 1969 Cup-Winners Cup.
4. Apart from Gary Lineker, only one other England player scored during the 1986 World Cup Finals - who was he?
5. Name the Scottish football team which plays at Rugby Park.
6. Which Football League club had considered joining the Scottish League before it reached the First Division in 1974?

QUIZ 100

1. Which team did Rangers defeat in the Skol Cup Finals of 1987 and 1988?
2. Which top star did West Ham bring back from Italian soccer in March 1987?
3. The first European Nations Cup competition was played between 1958 and 1960. Which country won the somewhat truncated tournment?
4. The top scorer in the 1970 World Cup was a German - what was his name.
5. Who was the female vocalist who sang on Northern Ireland's 1982 World Cup record?
6. Which number did German ace striker Gerd Muller like to wear in World Cup matches?

QUIZ 101

1. Who hit two goals in Nottingham Forest's 1989 Littlewoods Cup Final victory over Luton?
2. With which club did Pat Jennings begin his long and distinguished Football League career?
3. Which Polish side did Manchester City defeat in their European success of 1970?
4. Where did the Americas play the Rest of the World for the UNICEF Charity in 1986?
5. Why did Stockport change their strip of sky blue and white stripes with black shorts in 1982?
6. In the 1960s, which club was managed by Ted Bates?

QUIZ 102

1. Which is the oldest League club in Wales?
2. Who was the striker who joined Liverpool from Middlesbrough in 1982 but scored only four League goals for them before joining Sunderland in 1984?
3. Who was the 1988 European Footballer of the Year?
4. Who was England's first-ever World Cup captain?
5. What are the colours of Bradford City?
6. Which mustachioed Liverpool midfielder was the 1979-80 Footballer of the Year?

QUIZ 103

1. Which team beat Bon Accord 36-0 in 1885 - still a record score for a first-class match in Britain?
2. Full-back Arthur Albiston played internationally for which country?
3. Which famous club did Chelsea beat in Athens to lift the 1971 Cup-Winners Cup?
4. In which colour of strip does New Zealand play?
5. Comedian Freddie Starr is a fan of which of the Merseyside clubs?
6. Apart from Dundee, which other Scottish town has a team called 'United'?

QUIZ 104

1. West Ham beat which other London club to take the 1975 FA Cup?
2. Kenny Jackett plays international football with which country?
3. In which European country does Partizan Tirana play?
4. Name the member of Belgium's 1986 World Cup team who could have chosen to play for Italy.
5. Which Brazilian team plays in broad red and black hooped jerseys?
6. Which London ground had, until the late 1970s, the largest capacity of any Football League stadium?

QUIZ 105

1. Rangers won 8-1 away to which team in a 1980 Premier League match?
2. What was the nickname of William Ralph Dean who scored 60 goals for Everton in 1927-28?
3. Where did QPR play the home leg of their 1984 UEFA Cup tie with Partizan Belgrade?
4. Who was the Welsh international star of the 1950s known as 'The Gentle Giant'?
5. Which number did Pele always wear?
6. John Toshack and Malcolm Allison have both been manager at which Portuguese club?

QUIZ 106

1. Who was manager at Brighton when Bristol Rovers won 8-2 there in 1973?
2. Which Liverpool star surprisingly decided to quit football in May 1988?
3. Which Scottish team, in their third appearance in the Final, defeated Moscow Dynamo to take the 1972 Cup-Winners Cup?
4. How many caps did West Ham's Alan Devonshire win - 8, 18 or 28?
5. Who was the Millwall player, author of the famous football diary *Only a Game*?
6. What was the name of the ball specially designed by Adidas for the 1978 World Cup Finals?

QUIZ 107

1. How many of their 42 League games did Stoke City win in 1984-85?
2. For which Scottish Premier League side did young internationalist John Collins star during 1988-89?
3. Which Danish international weighs 14 stone and speaks English with a Scouse accent?
4. Which young Nottingham Forest defender made his England debut against Denmark in September 1988?
5. What are the colours of Norwich City?
6. Why did a linesman punch the referee during the Argentinian League match between Independiente and Sariento in 1982?

QUIZ 108

1. Name the Scottish striker who scored nine goals for Bournemouth against Margate in the 1971-72 FA Cup.
2. To which club did Liverpool pay £600,000 for Craig Johnston in 1981?
3. Which club won the East German championship in ten consecutive seasons from 1979?
4. Name the striker, then with Bournemouth, who scored for Northern Ireland in the 1986 World Cup Finals.
5. St Johnstone play in which Scottish town?
6. Which European club tournament has Liverpool never won?

QUIZ 109

1. Which current First Division boss has been in management the longest - all of 24 years?
2. Which League club signed Yugoslavian goalkeeper Petar Borota in 1979?
3. Oleg Blokhin's goal helped which team take the 1975 Cup-Winners Cup?
4. Which country eliminated England in the qualifying competition for the 1978 World Cup, despite losing 2-0 at Wembley?
5. What was the title of the official film of the 1982 World Cup in Spain?
6. Northern Ireland international David McCreery once played for an American team from Tulsa - what was its full name?

QUIZ 110

1. Name the two clubs which Brian Clough has steered to the Football League Championship.
2. For which English club did Scottish striker Mo Johnston score 23 League goals from 1983 to 1984?
3. Portuguese star Alves was famous for wearing what extra item of clothing while playing matches in Britain?
4. Which Spanish club did England play in a 1982 World Cup warm-up match?
5. What is the nickname often given to players continually named as substitute?
6. Which Midlands side went on a soccer tour of China in 1978?

QUIZ 111

1. Which club did Ian Porterfield manage to the Third Division Title in 1980-81?
2. In 1988-89, which Scottish club signed Dutchmen Theo Snelders and Willem Van der Ark?
3. Which Dutchman hit two goals to help Anderlecht defeat West Ham in the 1976 Cup-Winners Cup Final?
4. Who scored four goals for England against Spain in the Madrid friendly of 1987?
5. Why did Tommy Docherty change Chelsea's nickname from 'The Pensioners' to 'The Blues'?
6. From which town do the Rangers of the Vauxhall Conference come?

QUIZ 112

1. Who was the first £100,000 British footballer?
2. Former Arsenal player John Kosmina played against Scotland in 1985 - for which country?
3. Which European national side is supported by peaceful fans who call themselves 'The Roligans'?
4. Who was the Brazilian substitute who scorned a great chance to settle the 1986 World Cup quarter-final with France by missing a late penalty?
5. Which club plays at Upton Park?
6. Which Argentinian club had players imprisoned after an unruly World Club Championship match with AC Milan in 1969?

QUIZ 113

1. Who was the first British player to be sold for £1 million?
2. Striker Wayne Clarke has four elder brothers who all played League soccer. Name any two of them.
3. Where did Manchester United play the home leg of their 1977 European tie with St Etienne?
4. Which country scored the most Home International Championship goals from 1883 to 1984?
5. Who are 'The Rams'?
6. Who was the Manchester United star sent off in a 1968 World Club Championship match in Argentina?

QUIZ 114

1. Liverpool sold Kevin Keegan to which German club in 1977?
2. West Ham stalwart Billy Bonds began his career at which other London club?
3. Aston Villa beat which club to take the 1982 European Cup?
4. Two of the scorers in England's 2-1 Wembley victory over Scotland in 1986 later played together for Rangers. Name them.
5. Name the former soccer star who made a 'Shape Up and Dance' record with ex-Miss World Mary Stavin.
6. In 1983, which two teams did Robert Maxwell want to merge into 'Thames Valley Royals'?

QUIZ 115

1. Which club has won the most Scottish League Titles?
2. Who was the Leeds defender known for 'biting legs' with his tackles?
3. In which major Italian seaport does the Sampdoria club play?
4. What are the three colours of the Cameroons strip?
5. What Football League record did much-loaned goalkeeper Eric Nixon create in 1986-87?
6. Andy Beattie was the first occupant of which soccer hot-seat?

QUIZ 116

1. Which club has won the most Scottish Cups?
2. Name the Norwich midfielder who became the latest English-born recruit to the Eire squad when he made his debut against France in February 1989.
3. Which was the first team to win a European trophy in a penalty shoot-out?
4. Who was the Polish goalkeeper who, in 1973, helped knock England out of the World Cup despite being labelled a 'clown' by Brian Clough?
5. Describe the strip worn by Queen's Park Rangers.
6. What was the name of the special British tournament, won by Celtic, held to commemorate the crowning of the Queen in 1953?

QUIZ 117

1. Which team has won the Football League Championship most often?
2. Coventry's 1987 Cup Final skipper Brian Kilcline joined the Sky Blues from which club?
3. In July 1988, which Greek club paid a staggering £4.7 million to Eintracht Frankfurt for Hungarian midfielder Lajos Detari?
4. When England beat Scotland 5-1 at Wembley in 1975, which QPR player scored two of the goals?
5. The late Eric Morecambe was a director of which club?
6. With which club did ex-Liverpool boss Bob Paisley win a League Championship medal as a player?

QUIZ 118

1. Who guided Wolves to League Cup success in 1980, only a year after being seriously injured in a car crash?
2. Which former Liverpool player was known as 'Crazy Horse'?
3. Approximately, how many people paid to see the West Ham-Castilla Cup-Winners Cup clash in 1980?
4. Where do Northern Ireland play their home matches?
5. Name the Football League player famous for his white headband.
6. Which club has won the more League Championships - Newcastle or Sunderland?

QUIZ 119

1. What was the score in QPR's draw with Newcastle in 1984?
2. Who is thought to be England's first millionaire soccer-player?
3. Which club, from the Soviet Republic of Georgia, took the 1981 Cup-Winners Cup, defeating Carl Zeiss Jena in the Dusseldorf Final?
4. For which country does Ian Rush play his international football?
5. Where do home fans sing at the Gwladys Street End?
6. Name the referee of the first European Cup Final who also officiated in TV's 'It's a Knockout'.

QUIZ 120

1. Which English club has had the fewest managers since its formation?
2. For which Scotsman did Brian Clough pay £150,000 to Birmingham in 1977?
3. Which Danish star scored for Barcelona in their 1982 Cup-Winners Cup victory?
4. Who is Celtic's most capped player?
5. Which Second Division club has to·compete with two successful neighbouring Rugby League teams?
6. What variation on the off-side law was used in the North American Soccer League?

QUIZ 121

1. In which year did the first Football League substitute appear?
2. Who was the strong-running Manchester City and England midfielder known as 'Nijinsky' after the famous racehorse?
3. What advantage did Barcelona have when they defeated Standard Liege in the 1982 Cup-Winners Cup Final?
4. Which UEFA member nation did not compete in the 1986 World Cup?
5. Which is the only British senior football team whose name starts with the letter 'k'?
6. Who is the former Manchester United winger who, in 1984, became the League's youngest manager, at the age of 28?

QUIZ 122

1. Which of the original member clubs is not now in the Football League?
2. Who kept goal for Arsenal's Championship side of 1989?
3. Name the Spanish goalkeeper who allowed a Michel Platini free-kick to slip through his hands, giving France a crucial lead in the 1984 European Championship Final.
4. Has Chelsea's Graham Roberts ever been capped for England?
5. Which Scottish Premier League ground was the first all-seater stadium in Britain?
6. Billy McNeill's first managerial post was at which club?

QUIZ 123

1. How many clubs comprised the original line-up of the Football League?
2. England superstar Gary Lineker began his goal-scoring career at which Midlands club?
3. What is the rather unfortunate name of Bordeaux's French international goalkeeper?
4. In the 1986 World Cup, which team eliminated the hosts Mexico?
5. Dundee play in which colour of jersey?
6. Has Celtic ever won the European Cup-Winners Cup?

QUIZ 124

1. Which is the oldest Football League club?
2. Name the centre-half who won a UEFA Cup medal in 1973 and a European Cup medal in 1979 - with different clubs.
3. Where did Aberdeen defeat Real Madrid to take the 1983 Cup-Winners Cup?
4. Who was the winger, capped four times for England in 1976, while a Third Division player with Crystal Palace?
5. Who is the current Welsh international nicknamed 'Sparky'?
6. What is the name of the 110,000 capacity stadium in Mexico City?

QUIZ 125

1. Which is the oldest Scottish League club?
2. Arsenal signed John Lukic from which club in 1983?
3. Which Dutchman, later to play for Forest and Spurs, appeared for Real Madrid against Aberdeen in the 1983 Cup-Winners Cup Final?
4. Who was the Liverpool forward who played in England's World Cup-Winning XI?
5. Olympic athlete John Sherwood has a brother who has kept goal for Watford and Grimsby - what's his name?
6. For which club did John Bond play in the 1964 FA Cup Final?

QUIZ 126

1. Which team was the first to do the 'Double' of League and FA Cup?
2. Manchester United goalkeeper Jim Leighton won Scottish Premier League Championship medals with which club?
3. Which Portuguese club beat both Rangers and Aberdeen to reach the 1984 Cup-Winners Cup Final?
4. Name the Northern Ireland defender who was rather harshly sent off in the 1982 World Cup match with Spain.
5. Who were Liverpool's first shirt sponsors?
6. If a player hits the post with a penalty and then knocks the rebound into the net, what should the referee award?

QUIZ 127

1. In which decade was the first floodlit Football League match?
2. Which member of Liverpool's 1986 'Double' side once played for Inverness Caledonian?
3. Which League of Ireland side did Everton eliminate when they won the 1984-85 Cup-Winners Cup?
4. Who was the last member of England's 1966 World Cup team to retire from playing?
5. What was the nickname of Chelsea and England goalkeeper Peter Bonetti?
6. Celtic had only three managers between 1965 and 1989 - name them.

QUIZ 128

1. In which year were Manchester United involved in the tragic air crash at Munich?
2. Who kept goal for Rangers in the Skol Cup Finals of 1987 and 1988?
3. Where did Celtic replay their trouble-hit European tie with Rapid Vienna in 1984?
4. Before Peter Shilton, who was the last goalkeeper to captain England?
5. Which sportswear company supplied both the England and Scotland kits during 1989?
6. At which of the following can a player not be off-side - a direct free-kick, an indirect free-kick or a corner-kick?

QUIZ 129

1. For which club did the 'Busby Babes' play?
2. Who was the Sheffield Wednesday forward who had a leg amputated after being injured against Preston in 1953?
3. Whose own-goal cost Arsenal the home leg of their 1972 European Cup quarter-final with Ajax?
4. Who captained Brazil to World Cup glory in 1970, scoring himself in the Final with a superb low shot?
5. Southampton adopted which colours for their change strip in 1980?
6. Andy Gray has played in derby matches in Birmingham, Liverpool, Dundee and Glasgow. Name the clubs for which he played in these games.

QUIZ 130

1. What was new to the Football League in 1958?
2. John McClelland has played in two World Cups with which country?
3. Name the Dutchman whose two goals against his fellow countrymen of PSV Eindhoven helped Mechelen lift the 1989 European Super Cup.
4. Who made his England debut against Eire in 1980 while with West Bromwich Albion?
5. Which Welsh club spent £800,000 on a new stand in 1981?
6. Who was the PFA Player of the Year for 1988-89?

QUIZ 131

1. Which club had the 'Glory, Glory' team of the 1960s?
2. For which Football League club did Polish World Cup skipper Kazimierz Denya play?
3. Who was the first European Footballer of the Year, in 1956?
4. Which Dutch star was fouled in the first minute of the 1974 World Cup Final with West Germany?
5. What is the name of the home supporters end of Arsenal's Highbury stadium?
6. Who was the first footballer to be knighted?

QUIZ 132

1. What is the record number of draws in Division One on a single Saturday?
2. At the start of the 1988-89 season, defender Kevin Bond left Southampton to join which Second Division club?
3. Which Spanish club did Ron Atkinson manage for 94 days of the 1988-89 season?
4. Who was England's assistant-manager at the 1982 World Cup in Spain?
5. What is the profession of TV commentator Barry Davies?
6. Former Arsenal boss Don Howe managed which club from 1971 to 1974?

QUIZ 133

1. Who, in terms of honours won, is the most successful English League manager of all time?
2. Former Hearts assistant-boss Sandy Jardine played over 700 matches with which other top Scottish club?
3. Which Portuguese team play in Celtic-style jerseys?
4. Former Everton, Arsenal and Palace goalkeeper George Wood was an international cap for which country?
5. To which new town did Luton consider moving in 1983?
6. Which was the last major trophy won by Bill Shankly as Liverpool manager?

QUIZ 134

1. Which city had a team called 'Park Avenue' which was voted out of the League in 1970?
2. Who became Liverpool captain when Graeme Souness left to go to Italy in 1984?
3. In 1960, where did Real Madrid win their fifth consecutive European Cup, beating Eintracht Frankfurt 7-3?
4. Who scored from the penalty-spot to give Scotland victory over England at Wembley in 1981?
5. As well as Newcastle, which team has a ground called St James Park?
6. Which is the only Scottish club called 'City'?

QUIZ 135

1. Whom did Ron Atkinson succeed as Manchester United boss in June 1981?
2. Mick Coop was a long-serving defender with which club?
3. Who was the manager who left Bayern Munich in 1987 to take charge at Cologne?
4. Who crossed for Geoff Hurst to score the crucial, hotly disputed third goal in the 1966 World Cup Final?
5. Describe the strip of Newcastle United.
6. At which club did Dave Sexton take over after being sacked as Manchester United boss in 1981?

QUIZ 136

1. Who scored Everton's goals in their 2-0 FA Cup Final victory over Watford in 1984?
2. Which Football League star of the 1980s is a law graduate from Cordoba University?
3. Who compete for the European Super Cup?
4. Who was Scotland's manager in their inglorious 1978 World Cup campaign?
5. From which London club's ground could you watch the Boat Race?
6. Name a club other than Arsenal for which George Graham played.

QUIZ 137

1. In 1929, what was Newcastle United the first club to appoint?
2. Full-back Viv Anderson started out with which club?
3. Which Welsh club beat Malta's Sliema Wanderers 12-0 in a 1982 Cup-Winners Cup match?
4. What colour is the traditional change strip of West Germany?
5. To the nearest five minutes, what was the average time that the ball was in play during a 1986 World Cup match?
6. Arthur Cox lead Derby to promotion in 1987, but which club did he also take up in 1984?

QUIZ 138

1. Which of these clubs has spent the most seasons in the First Division - Arsenal, Everton or Manchester United?
2. Midfielder Tommy Burns has played over 300 matches for which club since 1975?
3. In which country were Dnepr champions for 1988?
4. What is Algeria's first choice strip colour?
5. Who said in 1985, when applying for the job of Eire team boss, 'It's easy to get to Ireland - just a walk across the sea for me'?
6. Who is the Chairman of the Football Association?

QUIZ 139

1. Which team took its name from a cricket club whose members were only free to play on their midweek half-day holiday?
2. For which Scottish club did Hamish McAlpine keep goal from 1969 to 1986?
3. Which Midlands team competed in the first four European Fairs Cups?
4. Name the two Arsenal full-backs who played together 29 times for Northern Ireland in the 1970s.
5. Which Football League club has had the most grounds?
6. What is a Sheffield Wednesday fan known as?

QUIZ 140

1. Which famous old club did Oxford United replace in the Football League in 1962?
2. Name the QPR central defender who played for Northern Ireland in the 1986 World Cup.
3. On which island would you watch Portuguese First Division side Maritimo play?
4. Who was Scotland's goalkeeper in the 1978 and 1982 World Cups?
5. Apart from being a good footballer, what would you have to be to play for Athletic Bilbao?
6. Who was assistant to Don Revie at Leeds and for England?

QUIZ 141

1. Which phrase was used to describe the playing-style of the Spurs team in the 1950s?
2. Northern Ireland international Sammy McIlroy appeared in three FA Cup Finals - with which team?
3. Which country's sides dominated the early years of the European Fairs Cup?
4. In 1961, what was the record score set up for an England victory over Scotland?
5. Who are 'The Potters'?
6. Which British city is the leading birthplace of Football League players?

QUIZ 142

1. What was the surname of the brothers who played together in Manchester United's 1977 Cup-winning side?
2. For which team did Steve McMahon play between leaving Everton and joining Liverpool?
3. Leeds United lost their first European Final in 1967 - to which Yugoslav club?
4. Who was captain of the 1986 World Cup runners-up West Germany?
5. Songwriter Andrew Lloyd-Weber and his brother Julian both follow which London club?
6. What was original about the Millwall-Fulham League match of January 1974?

QUIZ 143

1. Which was the first team to rise from the Fourth Division to the First?
2. International centre-half Alex McLeish has made over 300 appearances for which club?
3. From which country do the teams Aarhus and Vejle come?
4. In which year did Kenny Dalglish win his first cap - 1971, 1973 or 1975?
5. Which former England striker took part in a World Cup Rally to Mexico in 1970?
6. Which club has won the more League Titles - Arsenal or Tottenham?

QUIZ 144

1. Which team holds the record for an unbeaten home run in the Football League?
2. Who is the Scottish internationalist who left Celtic to join Borussia Dortmund in June 1987?
3. MTK play in which European country?
4. Who was the Leeds player, later manager of Bradford, who was sent off while playing for England against Argentina in 1977?
5. On which traditional song is the 'Match of the Day' theme tune based?
6. Which club did manager Joe Harvey guide to European Fairs Cup success in 1969?

QUIZ 145

1. Which top team beat Bristol Rovers 9-0 in October 1977, during a brief spell in the Second Division?
2. With which club did both Kevin Keegan and Ray Clemence begin their professional careers?
3. Ray Kennedy's away goal helped which English side lift the European Fairs Cup in 1970?
4. Name the Mexican striker who likes to salute his goals with a somersault.
5. Which club plays at Brunton Park?
6. In which League do Everton and Liverpool reserves play?

QUIZ 146

1. Which London side, managed by Terry Venables, was dubbed the 'Team of the Eighties' but never lived up to the expectations?
2. For which country was Blackpool's Tony Green an international in the 1970s?
3. In which German city would you find the Waldstadion?
4. Which FIFA member country has the largest number of registered players?
5. Describe the strip worn by Coventry in their victorious FA Cup Final appearance of 1987.
6. Does the team which wins the toss kick off?

QUIZ 147

1. Name the Scottish manager who guided Leicester City to the Second Division Title in 1980.
2. For which country was Terry Hennessey an international?
3. Who is the only Scotsman to have won the European Footballer of the Year award?
4. Harry Gregg kept goal for which country in the 1958 World Cup?
5. Which ground was the backdrop for L.S. Lowry's painting *Going to the Match*?
6. At which Spanish club did Jock Wallace take over after leaving Rangers in 1986?

QUIZ 148

1. At Stamford Bridge in May 1986, who scored the goal which clinched that year's League Championship for Liverpool?
2. At which club did George Best and Rodney Marsh play together in 1976?
3. Which Spanish club defeated Leeds United for the honour of keeping the old European Fairs Cup trophy?
4. Who is the President of FIFA?
5. What fate, according to Kevin Keegan, often became of England manager Don Revie's dossiers on the opposition?
6. Name the former Middlesbrough goalkeeper who won 23 Northern Ireland caps between 1976 and 1986.

QUIZ 149

1. Who took over as Manchester City manager on the departure of Billy McNeill in September 1986?
2. Which striker was the subject of two £1 million-plus deals in 1980?
3. In 1972, which fellow English side did Spurs defeat in the first UEFA Cup Final?
4. Who was the top goalscorer in the 1986 World Cup Tournament in Mexico?
5. Which club plays at Tannadice Park?
6. What were re-adopted by the Football League in 1986-87, after an absence of 89 years?

QUIZ 150

1. In 1981-82, what change was made in the Football League to encourage attacking play?
2. Test cricketer Denis Compton played 32 League games for which club between 1946 and 1949?
3. Which German side have Liverpool beaten in two European competition finals?
4. Who were the first Home International Champions?
5. Who are 'The Latics' from Boundary Park?
6. What was untimely about Wigan Borough's resignation from the Football League in 1931?

QUIZ 151

1. What change was made in 1976-77 in the way League positions were decided?
2. Who was stripped of the West Ham captaincy following a breach of discipline before an FA Cup defeat at Blackpool in 1971?
3. In which city did Leeds fans riot after losing the 1975 European Cup Final to Bayern Munich?
4. Name the only country to play in the final stages of every World Cup between 1930 and 1986.
5. What is the traditional shirt colour of Preston North End?
6. What incentive was given to the League Cup Finalists from 1967 onwards?

QUIZ 152

1. Which club holds the record for the longest run without a win in a Football League season?
2. Rangers signed striker Ally McCoist from which English club in 1983?
3. Which strip colour is common to Rapid Vienna, Ferencvaros and Panathinaikos?
4. Who was the Argentinian defender, with the English-sounding surname, who headed the opening goal in the 1986 World Cup Final?
5. Greenock is home to which Scottish League club?
6. By what name was the Vauxhall-Opel League formerly known?

QUIZ 153

1. Arsenal, Aston Villa and Stoke - which of these clubs was not an original Football League member?
2. Long-term injury victim Jim Beglin is an international with which country?
3. Who scored from a free-kick in Bruges to clinch the 1976 UEFA Cup for Liverpool?
4. Name either of the two Arsenal players in England's 1982 World Cup side.
5. Which manager sued both his former player Willie Morgan and Granada Television for libel in 1978?
6. Who was the former Charlton striker who was voted the North American Soccer League's Most Valuable Player in 1978?

QUIZ 154

1. Which First Division club of 1982-83 had, by 1986, slumped into the Fourth?
2. Name the Rangers and England star who was born in Singapore.
3. Which European capital has a team called AEK?
4. Which club supplied six of the England team for Ron Greenwood's first match as manager in September 1977?
5. What is the usual away strip of Manchester United?
6. In which country, in 1964, were over 300 people killed in the World's worst-ever football stadium disaster?

QUIZ 155

1. Which club was elected to the Football League in 1977?
2. Who was the Sunderland full-back signed by Liverpool in 1986 after writing to inform Kenny Dalglish of his availability?
3. Which striker scored two goals for Spurs in the first leg of the all-English UEFA Cup Final of 1972?
4. Name the German who scored in the Final of both the 1974 and 1982 World Cups.
5. Who was elected Chairman of the Professional Footballers' Association in 1956?
6. Name the former Birmingham winger who is presently Chief Executive of the PFA.

QUIZ 156

1. Which team won the 1961-62 League Championship in its first season in Division One?
2. Derby signed which Welsh international striker from Oxford in October 1988?
3. What was remarkable about the line-up for the semi-finals of the 1980 UEFA Cup?
4. Which country had a player called Muller in its 1986 World Cup squad?
5. In 1890, which football item did Mr Brodie of Liverpool invent to help settle arguments about goal or no goal?
6. If a player is shown a yellow card by the referee, what does this mean?

QUIZ 157

1. Which team, in 1985, won its first thirteen Division Three matches?
2. Name the tall Scottish international goalkeeper bought by Dundee United from St Mirren in 1984.
3. Ipswich lifted the 1981 UEFA Cup in a thrilling final against which Dutch team?
4. Which country won the first World Cup in 1930?
5. In which colour of strip does Millwall play?
6. Which British manager guided Al-Nasr to victory in the 1987 Saudi Arabian Kings Cup?

QUIZ 158

1. Which First Division club went unbeaten in 42 League matches from November 1977 to December 1978?
2. For which country did former Oldham and West Bromwich forward Carl Valentine play in the 1986 World Cup?
3. Which British team lost the 1966 European Cup-Winners Cup Final to Borussia Dortmund at Hampden?
4. Manchester United's Johnny Carey played internationally for two countries - name them.
5. In a 1964 match against Bury, who was the Manchester City goalkeeper who went into the forward-line and scored the equalizer for City?
6. How many Laws of the Game are there?

QUIZ 159

1. Which Cumbrian club did Wimbledon replace in the Football League?
2. In between two spells at Nottingham Forest, Garry Birtles had a relatively lean two seasons as a striker with which major club?
3. In 1988-89, which city had representatives in the quarter-finals of all three European tournaments?
4. In the famous World Cup match of 1973, when Poland drew 1-1 at Wembley to qualify, who scored England's goal?
5. Which club has been known as both 'Black Arabs' and 'Eastville Rovers'?
6. Liverpool were trounced in the 1981 World Club Championship by which Brazilian side?

QUIZ 160

1. Which team did Cambridge United replace in the Football League in 1970?
2. Which was Chris Waddle's first club?
3. Gothenburg shocked which top German club with a 3-0 away win in the 1982 UEFA Cup Final second leg?
4. Who was the Dutchman who scored for both sides in the crunch 1978 World Cup match against Italy?
5. Who are 'The Shakers' from Gigg Lane?
6. What did 'North and South' become in 1958?

QUIZ 161

1. Which London club has played in Division One since 1919?
2. Which England international was captain of Chelsea at the age of 18?
3. In the 1950s, which English team played a series of floodlit friendlies against continental opposition which provided a stimulus for a European Cup competition?
4. Who is the goalkeeper who made his England debut against the USA in 1985?
5. In 1958, which club first used an 'electric blanket' to beat frost?
6. Which club has won the more Sheffield derby matches - United or Wednesday?

QUIZ 162

1. In 1972, Hereford United replaced which Northern team in the Football League?
2. Who is the midfielder who joined Nottingham Forest from Portsmouth for £275,000 in 1985?
3. Name the striker who was voted West Germany's 1988 Footballer of the Year while playing for VfB Stuttgart.
4. Teofilo Cubillas starred in the 1970 and 1978 World Cups for which country?
5. In the 1960s, Don Revie based the Leeds strip on the outfit of which famous club?
6. From which sport is the term hat-trick borrowed?

QUIZ 163

1. Which Tyneside club lost its League place to Peterborough United in 1960?
2. Goalkeeper Pat Bonner, who joined Celtic in 1978, is an international with which country?
3. Which Spanish side defeated both Rangers and Arsenal in winning the 1980 Cup-Winners Cup?
4. Against which European country did Scotland gain their only victory in the 1978 World Cup Finals?
5. What are West Ham popularly called?
6. Which Russian club made a famous tour of Britain in 1945?

QUIZ 164

1. In 1978, which was the last team to lose its League status by unsuccessfully applying for re-election?
2. Which was Everton centre-half Dave Watson's first League club?
3. Which English club knocked Celtic out of the 1983-84 UEFA Cup when Colin Walsh scored the winner at Parkhead?
4. Name either of .the England players who scored in both the 1966 and 1970 World Cup tournaments.
5. Who was known as 'El Tel'?
6. Which league was first sponsored by Beazer Homes in 1987-88?

QUIZ 165

. 1. Which team were the first Football League Champions in 1889?
2. Who was the Celtic and Scotland winger forced to retire early due to a prolonged viral illness?
3. In 1968, both the English and European Footballer of the Year awards were won by the same Manchester United star. Who was he?
4. Which country ended Northern Ireland's gallant 1982 World Cup run by beating them 4-1 in Madrid?
5. Which Scottish town is home to East Stirling?
6. Who was the Spurs star elected Footballer of the Year for 1981-82?

QUIZ 166

1. Joe Mercer guided which team to the League Title in 1967-68?
2. Which club sold midfielder David Armstrong to Southampton in 1981?
3. Which city in Eastern Europe has teams named Bohemians, Slavia and Sparta?
4. What colour was England's change strip for the 1986 World Cup Finals?
5. Which ITV commentator once said 'He had an eternity to play that ball - but he took too long'?
6. What is the maximum weight allowed for the ball at the start of a match?

QUIZ 167

1. Which club did former Arsenal player Ted Drake lead to the League Title in 1955?
2. Name Tottenham's 1982 signing from Bristol Rovers who has played for England at Youth, Under-21 and Full International levels.
3. Name the goalkeeper whose save in the penalty shoot-out won the 1984 UEFA Cup for Tottenham.
4. Which country's badge now features the Jules Rimet Trophy?
5. In their formative years, when Arsenal were hard-up, which club lent them a spare red and white kit - the colours of which they have worn ever since?
6. Name three Football League clubs called 'Rovers'.

QUIZ 168

1. In August 1988, Rangers recorded their biggest victory over arch-rivals Celtic for 25 years. What was the score?
2. Which defender did Manchester United sign from League of Ireland side St Patrick's Athletic in 1982?
3. Which German World Cup star brought down Kevin Keegan to give Liverpool the vital penalty in the 1977 European Cup Final?
4. Who was the Southampton winger who scored on his debut for England against Egypt in Cairo in 1986?
5. To the nearest 5 stone, what was the weight of Fatty Foulke who played for Sheffield United and Chelsea in the early part of this century?
6. Which French side are known by the initials PSG?

QUIZ 169

1. Name the management duo who led Coventry to FA Cup triumph in 1987.
2. Which striker began his second spell with West Ham after signing from Celtic in March 1989?
3. Which two British 'Uniteds' clashed in the 1984-85 UEFA Cup - and who won?
4. Which European country plays in red shirts, blue shorts and black socks with red and yellow trims?
5. D.J. David Hamilton and singer Ralph McTell are both fans of which team?
6. Name the three members of Forest's 1978 Championship squad who had previously won a League medal with Derby in 1972.

QUIZ 170

1. Who managed Aston Villa's Championship-winning side of 1980-81?
2. With which club did veteran Tommy Hutchison win all of his 17 Scottish caps?
3. A team from a neighbouring country ended Real Madrid's run of European Cup wins by taking the trophy in 1961 - which team?
4. Who scored a great solo goal for England against Brazil in Rio, 1984?
5. During the 1958 World Cup, which Irishman said his tactics were 'to equalize before the other team score'?
6. In a 1951 Third Division match, what was unusual about Stockport forwards Alec Herd and David Herd?

QUIZ 171

1. Who managed Everton's Championship side of 1970?
2. Which player joined Manchester United from West Bromwich at the same time as Bryan Robson?
3. Which Scottish striker has, in recent seasons, scored UEFA Cup goals against Inter-Milan, Barcelona and Bayern Munich?
4. In which Mexican city did England play their 1970 World Cup group matches?
5. Which unusual colour did Coventry adopt for their change strip in the early 1980s?
6. In 1974, who became the first British players ever to be sent off at Wembley?

QUIZ 172

1. Who was manager of Arsenal's 'Double' side of 1970-71?
2. Which club sold John Aldridge to Liverpool in 1987?
3. What is the famous strip of Real Madrid?
4. Who is England's most-capped goalkeeper?
5. Which Scottish League team plays at Cliftonhill Park, Coatbridge?
6. Of which club is former Arsenal boss Bertie Mee now a director?

QUIZ 173

1. Which North-Eastern club played for 68 successive seasons in Division One before being relegated in 1958?
2. Name the Everton and Scotland right-winger with left-wing views and a trendy taste in fashion.
3. Which top European club is often known by the letters HSV?
4. What is the distinctive feature of the Peru strip?
5. Why was a white horse called Billy a hero of the 1923 FA Cup Final?
6. How many fans are estimated to have crammed in to watch the 1923 West Ham-Bolton Cup Final?

QUIZ 174

1. Which Scottish Premier League club has been managed by Ally MacLeod, Jimmy Bonthrone and Billy McNeill?
2. From which club did Luton sign striker Mick Harford?
3. Name the Argentinian forward who struck twice for Real Madrid in their UEFA Cup Final win over Cologne in 1986.
4. Which country played no internationals on home soil from October 1971 to March 1975?
5. How did Argentinian fans welcome their team onto the field during the 1978 World Cup?
6. Who are the Associate Members of the Football League?

QUIZ 175

1. Which club won the Second Division, First Division, FA Cup, League Cup and Cup-Winners Cup in the space of four years from 1966 to 1970?
2. What was the nationality of Nottingham Forest's 1981 signing Einar Aas?
3. Which club reached three consecutive European Cup-Winners Cup Finals in the 1970s?
4. Who was the goalkeeper who played five times for Wales in 1972-73 but made only one League appearance for his club, Leeds United?
5. Which Irish League club plays at Solitude?
6. In the 1950s, which successful team was managed by Stan Cullis?

QUIZ 176

1. In 1970, which team was in contention for the treble of League, FA Cup and European Cup, but ended up missing out on all three?
2. From which club did Arsenal sign Perry Groves in 1986?
3. Which current British manager scored a tremendous European Cup hat-trick for Liverpool against CSKA Sofia in 1981?
4. In the 1986 World Cup, who took over as Scotland captain when Graeme Souness was dropped?
5. Former Labour leader Michael Foot is a fan of which West Country side?
6. Where is the *Copa Libertadores* contested?

QUIZ 177

1. In 1972, which team were pipped by one point of the 'Double' when they lost their last League match to Wolves?
2. Goalkeeper Eddie Niedzwiecki was a full international for which country?
3. Which was the last British side to win a European trophy?
4. Which top club had at least one player capped for England in every season from 1946 to 1971?
5. What colour is worn by Raith Rovers, St Johnstone and Stranraer?
6. Which Football League club has the shortest name?

QUIZ 178

1. In 1974, which team did Jackie Charlton manage to a Second Division Title, by a then record 15 points margin?
2. 1988-89 Chelsea star Peter Nicholas has been much capped by which of the home nations?
3. Who are the only British team to lose a European tie with a four-goal first-leg advantage?
4. In 1950, England were involved in a World Cup sensation when they lost 1-0 to which unfashionable soccer nation?
5. How many times was the Inverness Thistle-Falkirk Scottish Cup tie postponed in 1979 - 9, 19 or 29?
6. Name the famous ticket tout who is chairman of Barnet.

QUIZ 179

1. Of which competition were Small Heath the first winners?
2. Which ex-Manchester United and Northern Ireland defender helped Rangers win the Scottish League in 1987?
3. In 1981, which Scottish club went to Monte Carlo and defeated Monaco 5-2 in a UEFA Cup match watched by Prince Rainier?
4. How many goals did Nat Lofthouse score for the English League against the League of Ireland in 1952?
5. In 1950, when Greece became the first country to introduce 3-points-for-a-win, two points were awarded for a draw - but for what was one point awarded?
6. Which of these Yorkshire clubs has won the most League Championships - Leeds, Barnsley or Huddersfield?

QUIZ 180

1. Who succeeded Bob Paisley as Liverpool manager in 1983?
2. Celtic signed defender Mick McCarthy from which English club in 1987?
3. Name the QPR player who scored a hat-trick in both legs of the UEFA Cup tie with Brann Bergen in 1976.
4. Who was the Manchester United player who scored for England in three consecutive matches against Scotland from 1978 to 1980?
5. What are Melchester's colours in the Roy of the Rovers comic?
6. What was the maximum points total in the 1988-89 First Division?

--------------------------------- **QUIZ 181** ---------------------------------

1. Which unenviable 'first' did Lincoln City become in 1987?
2. For which country was Terry Mancini an international?
3. How many of the Liverpool team scored in their 1974 UEFA Cup match with Stromgodset of Norway?
4. Who won the first Rous Cup in 1985?
5. At which ground is the massive Holte End?
6. Celtic's 1983 Scottish Footballer of the Year returned North in 1987, after four years in England. Can you name him?

--------------------------------- **QUIZ 182** ---------------------------------

1. In 1988-89, which team played Division One football for the first time?
2. Goalkeeper Steve Ogrizovic was once on the books of which of the Merseyside clubs?
3. In which country do teams compete in the *Bundesliga*?
4. Who were the last Home International Champions?
5. Which club's badge features a cockerel?
6. Which League club has had its ground closed most often due to fans' misbehaviour?

--------------------------------- **QUIZ 183** ---------------------------------

1. Which British football manager was knighted in 1968?
2. Roy Dwight, who scored for Forest against Luton in the 1959 Cup Final was the cousin of which famous pop star?
3. Name the German striker who lifted the 1980 and 1981 European Footballer of the Year awards.
4. How did the Russian Tofik Bakhramov bring ecstasy to England fans in 1966?
5. Which club does TV presenter Des Lynam support?
6. In which Asian City is the World Club Championship decider played?

QUIZ 184

1. Which team won the inaugural Milk Cup Tournament in 1983?
2. Name the striker bought by Manchester City from Norwich for over £1 million in March 1980.
3. Which British club has made the most appearances in European competitions?
4. What was the score when Scotland played England at Hampden in the SFA Centenary match of 1973?
5. A fan of which club might shout 'Play up Pompey'?
6. Which current League manager was blacklisted by Scotland after comments made while in the squad during the 1978 World Cup shambles in Argentina?

QUIZ 185

1. In 1967, which club did the unique double of Third Division Championship and Football League Cup?
2. Martin O'Neill was with which club when he starred for Northern Ireland in the 1982 World Cup?
3. Kevin Hector knocked in five UEFA Cup goals against Finn Harps in 1976 - with which club was he playing?
4. Which midfielder was Scotland's top scorer in the 1982 World Cup Finals?
5. In the TV series starring Adam Faith, 'Budgie' supported which club?
6. Who was the high-scoring Ipswich midfielder voted the Players' Player of the Year in 1981?

QUIZ 186

1. What feature did the FA Cup Finals of 1967, 1975 and 1980 have in common?
2. Steve Hunt was a goalscoring sensation in which country before starring in the English First Division with Coventry City?
3. Name any of the three English clubs which have won the Fairs/UEFA Cup twice.
4. Who was the blond Northern Ireland striker of the 1970s who played for Bury, Blackpool and Greek club Olympiakos?
5. Which Scottish First Division side plays in a white strip with a red diamond?
6. Four clubs in the 1988-89 Second Division had, at one time, been holders of a European trophy - name any two of them.

QUIZ 187

1. Who captained Rangers in their victorious Scottish League campaigns of 1986-87 and 1988-89?
2. Paul Power played 365 League matches for which club, before joining Everton in 1986?
3. Which team beat Rangers to win the first European Super Cup in 1973?
4. By what name is Brazilian Artur Antunes Coimbra better known?
5. What were the colours of ill-fated Newport County?
6. Who is the former Wolves boss who has managed Notts County and Walsall in recent seasons?

QUIZ 188

1. Which team reached both the League Cup and FA Cup Finals in 1982?
2. Name the QPR and West Ham goalkeeper who advertised 'Cossack' men's hairspray.
3. Which British city had teams in both the European Cup Final and the Cup-Winners Cup Final in 1967?
4. Name the Aston Villa midfielder, who scored England's second goal in their 2-0 Wembley victory over Scotland in 1983.
5. Complete this well-known football manager's phrase - 'Sick as a ......?
6. Name the trophy awarded to the top European goalscorer.

QUIZ 189

1. Name either of the two teams which have defeated Liverpool in a League Cup Final.
2. From which club did Nottingham Forest sign Stuart Pearce in June 1985?
3. Which Scottish team beat European Champions Hamburg to lift the 1983 European Super Cup?
4. Whom did Mike England succeed as Wales manager?
5. Which player hired a private detective to find details of his grandfather which enabled him to qualify for the Republic of Ireland?
6. Can a corner-flag be any height?

QUIZ 190

1. Who were the first winners of the Football League Cup in 1961?
2. Oldham bought striker Roger Palmer from which neighbouring club in 1980?
3. Which Spanish team beat Forest in the 1980 European Super Cup?
4. Which South America country did England convincingly beat 3-0 in their 1986 World Cup second round match in Mexico City?
5. Who is the top football journalist who writes for The Sunday Times?
6. Who is the former Brighton and Luton player who succeeded Mark Lawrenson as Oxford United boss during 1988-89?

QUIZ 191

1. Which team has won the League Cup most often - Aston Villa, Liverpool or Norwich?
2. Stylish defender Russell Osman enjoyed European success with which team in 1981?
3. Hamburg and Liverpool drew 1-1 in the first leg of the European Super Cup in 1977 - what was the score in the second leg at Anfield?
4. Describe Argentina's national strip.
5. To which winger did Tommy Docherty say - 'Your deceptive - you're even slower than you look'?
6. Which team did Tommy Docherty twice take to Wembley during the 1970s?

QUIZ 192

1. Two Martin Chivers goals won which team the 1971 League Cup?
2. Which former Aston Villa winger scored for Den Haag in the 1987 Dutch Cup Final?
3. Which Italian World Cup star was voted the 1982 European Footballer of the Year?
4. What colour is Brazil's second choice jersey?
5. Which manager once said 'anything from 1-0 to 2-0 would be a nice result'?
6. Which Football League club was owned by the Bhatti brothers?

QUIZ 193

1. Ray Graydon's goal won the 1975 League Cup for which team?
2. Which former England striker was famous for his windmill-arm scoring celebration?
3. In which European country is there a football and sports magazine called *Kicker*?
4. Who was the Derby County player who was captain of Scotland's 1978 World Cup team?
5. What are the colours of Watford?
6. During the 1977-78 season, Manchester United signed two Scottish internationals from Leeds - name them.

QUIZ 194

1. Which team won the 1972 League Cup - its first major trophy in 109 years?
2. Did Juventus make a profit or loss on Ian Rush when they sold him back to Liverpool in August 1988?
3. Where was the 1987 European Super Cup match between Steaua Bucharest and Dynamo Kiev played?
4. Which top Dutch star was missing from their 1978 World Cup squad because of his premature retirement from international football?
5. Which Scottish ground underwent a £10 million re-development from 1978 to 1981?
6. What was different about promotion and relegation in the 1973-74 season?

QUIZ 195

1. Which team reached both the Milk Cup and FA Cup Finals in 1984?
2. Which First Division club signed former England Under-21 striker Paul Rideout from Italian side Bari in the summer of 1988?
3. Rosenborg Trondheim play in which Scandanavian country?
4. Who was captain of Argentina's 1978 World Cup-winning side?
5. For which film was the female lead given soccer lessons by Partick Thistle?
6. What age was the youngest-ever Football League player, Albert Geldard of Bradford Park Avenue?

QUIZ 196

1. Name the Liverpool player who scored in the League Cup Finals of 1982 and 1983.
2. At which top club did veteran goalkeeper Jimmy Rimmer begin his career?
3. Which World Cup star scored two goals for Juventus when they beat Liverpool 2-0 in Turin in the 1984 Super Cup game?
4. Name the midfield star of France's 1982 World Cup team who is only 5ft 3½ins in height.
5. Who are 'The Mariners' of Blundell Park?
6. Which is the only English football club with shares listed on the Stock Exchange?

QUIZ 197

1. Of which tournament were Wanderers the first winners?
2. Which player, capped 76 times by England, came out of retirement to play for Belfast Distillery in a 1963 European Cup tie?
3. Which famous Portuguese club are nicknamed 'The Eagles'?
4. For which country did Espanol goalkeeper Thomas N'Kono play in the 1982 World Cup?
5. What is the title of France's leading monthly football magazine?
6. How many games does it take to win the European Cup?

QUIZ 198

1. Name the goalkeeper who won League Cup medals in 1978 and 1985 with different clubs.
2. Former Everton and England midfielder Peter Reid began his career at which club?
3. Which famous Dutch club play in red and white halved shirts and black shorts?
4. In the 1966 World Cup, which country inflicted Brazil's first defeat in the tournament for twelve years?
5. Why was there a 22-way tie for Scottish Footballer of the Year in 1974?
6. Who was the Morton star voted 1979 Scottish Footballer of the Year?

QUIZ 199

1. For which team did Andy Gray's goal win the 1980 League Cup?
2. For which former Evertonian did Arsenal pay Watford £200,000 in August 1987?
3. Which top Italian side play in blue and black striped shirts?
4. England's 1966 World Cup goalkeeper Gordon Banks was with which club at that time?
5. Comedian Eddie Large is a staunch supporter of which team?
6. What is the top non-League side from Shropshire?

QUIZ 200

1. Brian Little's two goals helped which team win the League Cup in 1977?
2. With which club did veteran Scottish goalkeeper Alan Rough play for 13 years before joining Hibernian in 1982?
3. Dukla Prague play in which colour of jerseys?
4. Which South American country shattered Scotland's 1978 World Cup hopes by beating them 3-1 in their first match?
5. Which London club has its local Tube Station named after it?
6. What is the difference between the Irish League and the League of Ireland?

QUIZ 201

1. Who captained Wolves when they last won the League Cup?
2. To which club did Liverpool pay £300,000 for Ian Rush in 1980?
3. The shirts of French side Bordeaux are which colour?
4. Name the Leeds striker who scored a diving header to defeat Czechoslovakia and take Scotland into the 1974 World Cup Finals.
5. Who are 'The Posh'?
6. What was unusual about the goal scored by Aston Villa full-back Peter Aldis from 35 yards in 1952?

QUIZ 202

1. Who managed Oxford United to Milk Cup success in 1986?
2. England international winger Laurie Cunningham began his career at which club?
3. What colour of shirts do Red Star Belgrade wear?
4. Who was the moustachioed Brazilian free-kick specialist who played in three World Cups during the 1970s?
5. Why was Ipswich manager Bobby Robson outraged at Alan Hudson's goal for Chelsea in September 1970?
6. Which club did Stanley Matthews manage after he retired from playing?

QUIZ 203

1. Which team won the League Cup in 1969, but were prevented from competing in Europe because they were not a First Division side?
2. In 1978, which former Liverpool star gave Ossie Ardiles a personal demonstration of the toughness of the English League?
3. Who scored both goals for West Ham in their 1965 Cup-Winners Cup victory at Wembley?
4. Walter Schachner was a World Cup star for which country?
5. 'Follow Follow' is a traditional anthem for fans of which Scottish club?
6. Have European or South American clubs won the World Club Championship more often?

QUIZ 204

1. Who missed a penalty for Sunderland in the 1985 Milk Cup Final?
2. Scottish international Billy Liddell was a great favourite on Merseyside - at which club?
3. Name the Portuguese side from Oporto who play in unusual-style black and white checked jerseys.
4. Who beat holders Argentina in the first game of the 1982 World Cup Tournament in Spain?
5. What was the uncomplementary name given to England's group in the 1986 World Cup?
6. In which month does the Football League programme usually begin?

QUIZ 205

1. Which team reached three consecutive League Cup Finals from 1978 to 1980?
2. Who kept goal for Ipswich from 1975 to 1987?
3. What are the colours of Bayern Munich?
4. Which other South American country did Brazilian World Cup veteran Didi manage in the 1970 Tournament?
5. Name Devon's three Football League clubs.
6. Which manager once said 'I've had more clubs than Jack Nicklaus'?

QUIZ 206

1. Who hit the shot which was deflected into the Sunderland goal to win the 1985 Milk Cup for Norwich?
2. Danish star John Sivebaek was signed by which top English club in 1986?
3. Leeds won their second Fairs Cup in 1971 - beating which Italian side?
4. Which Dutchman played the 1978 World Cup Final with his arm in plaster?
5. Who is the controversial chairman of Chelsea?
6. Why were Glasgow Rangers unable to defend the European Cup-Winners Cup, won in 1972, in the following season's competition?

QUIZ 207

1. Who led Swansea City from the Fourth Division to the First from 1978 to 1981?
2. Name the striker signed by Everton from Dumbarton in 1980.
3. What are the colours of Hajduk Split?
4. Who were 'The Camels' who lost 1-0 to England in the 1982 World Cup?
5. Which TV football presenter took over from an injured linesman during the Arsenal-Liverpool match of September 1972?
6. Who is the former Newcastle and Nottingham Forest full-back who became boss of Orient in 1982?

QUIZ 208

1. Whose goal eventually settled the 1984 all-Merseyside Milk Cup Final in a replay at Maine Road?
2. In September 1988, who scored his first goal for Spurs despite having a boot missing?
3. Who was the Manchester United striker who celebrated his 19th birthday with a goal in the European Cup Final?
4. Which country did Scotland beat in a two-leg supplementary play-off to qualify for the 1986 World Cup?
5. What is the nickname of Jim Smith who became Newcastle boss in 1988?
6. Which First Division team did Howard Wilkinson manage from 1983 to 1988 before leaving to take over Leeds United?

QUIZ 209

1. Which of England's 1966 World Cup team took over in goal for West Ham in a 1972 League Cup replay with Stoke?
2. Which team bought Gordon Strachan from Manchester United in 1989?
3. What are the colours of Dublin side Bohemians?
4. Which country allowed Argentina to score six goals against them and so pip Brazil for a place in the 1978 World Cup Final?
5. What is the name of Cardiff City's home ground?
6. Who was the 1978 Footballer of the Year from Nottingham Forest?

QUIZ 210

1. Name the goalkeeper who established a British record 1196 minute shut-out during 1986-87.
2. Who was the goalkeeper who played his second senior game for Aston Villa in the 1982 European Cup Final?
3. 1988 Swedish champions Malmo play in which colour shirts?
4. In which year's World Cup Finals was the system of referee's yellow and red cards first used?
5. Which top player was known to team-mates as 'Mooro'?
6. Which banking group took over sponsorship of the Football League in 1987?

QUIZ 211

1. How many different nationalities were in Newcastle's 1952 FA Cup-winning team?
2. To which club did Arsenal pay £800,000 for striker Alan Smith in 1987?
3. Which Scottish team knocked holders Ipswich out of the 1981-82 UEFA Cup?
4. Which key player missed England's crunch 1970 World Cup quarter-final with West Germany because of a stomach bug?
5. Alphabetically, which is the first Football League club?
6. Which of the European competitions has never been won by a Scottish club?

QUIZ 212

1. Who captained Tottenham's 1981 and 1982 Cup-winning sides?
2. Who is the striker, nicknamed 'Inchy', who played in the 1988-89 Spanish League?
3. In winning the 1978-79 European Cup, which fellow British team did Nottingham Forest eliminate in Round One?
4. In 1966, Alf Ramsey prevented England players from swopping jerseys after a rough-house World Cup match with which South Americans?
5. Which team made a recording of 'Here We Go!' in 1985?
6. If a defender pulls an attacker's shirt in the penalty-box, what should the referee award?

QUIZ 213

1. Arsenal lifted the 1987 Littlewoods Cup thanks to two goals from which striker?
2. What is the name of Gary Mabbutt's older brother who played for Bristol City and Crystal Palace?
3. Describe Barcelona's jersey
4. Which Polish player hit a tremendous hat-trick against Belgium in the 1982 World Cup?
5. Which manager sang the praises of alcohol-free lager?
6. Which Argentinian club beat Celtic in a bruising 1967 World Club Championship match?

QUIZ 214

1. Noel Cantwell captained which team to FA Cup victory in 1963?
2. Which French World Cup star played for Aston Villa in 1984-85?
3. Which top continental team are sometimes referred to as 'The Zebras'?
4. Who was the Portuguese midfielder who shocked England in the 1986 World Cup by scoring the only goal of the match 15 minutes from time?
5. Which two British soccer clubs have the closest grounds to each other?
6. What did the beaten FA Cup semi-finalists do for a time during the 1970s?

QUIZ 215

1. Arsenal's 'Double' captain of 1971, Frank McLintock, had previously lost FA Cup Finals in 1961 and 1963 - with which team?
2. In which country was John Barnes born?
3. Describe the strip worn by Ajax Amsterdam.
4. Enzo Francescoli was one of the more skillful players for which country during the 1986 World Cup?
5. Michael Parkinson co-wrote the biography of which top soccer star?
6. Name either of the League clubs which Frank McLintock managed before becoming assistant to John Docherty at Millwall.

QUIZ 216

1. Tragedy-hit Manchester United still managed to reach the 1958 FA Cup Final - but which other Lancashire team beat them 2-0 at Wembley?
2. Who is Dundee United's veteran forward known as 'Luggie'?
3. Which was the first team from Eastern Europe to win the European Cup?
4. Which London club supplied three members of England's 1966 World Cup-winning side?
5. Who was the St Johnstone defender booked by referee Don McVicar during a 1987 match with Meadowbank?
6. What is the maximum length of a football pitch?

QUIZ 217
---

1. In 1972, which team, then in the Southern League, knocked Newcastle United out of the FA Cup?
2. For which top Scottish clubs did Pat Stanton star in the 1970s?
3. In what colour of shirts do Napoli play?
4. What nationality was referee Gottfried Dienst who awarded England their controversial third goal in the World Cup Final of 1966?
5. Who presented Grandstand's 'Football Preview' slot?
6. What was the name of the leading American club backed by Warner Communications?

QUIZ 218
---

1. Who is the only player to have twice captained West Ham to FA Cup victory?
2. What height is England defender Terry Butcher?
3. Which top Swiss team wear Blackburn Rovers style jerseys?
4. Who was the midfielder, then with Nottingham Forest, who scored a tremendous solo goal for Scotland against Holland in the 1978 World Cup?
5. Which top manager was best man at George Graham's wedding and played against him later that day?
6. How many British teams have won the World Club Championship?

QUIZ 219
---

1. What was Matthew Betts of Wanderers the first player to do?
2. Name the midfielder who won a Scottish Cup medal in 1984 and an FA Cup medal the following year.
3. Which club from a rich principality plays in the French League in red and white diagonally-halved shirts?
4. Who missed a penalty for Italy in the 1982 World Cup Final?
5. Which Irish League side plays at Windsor Park?
6. In April 1985, which then Fourth Division manager was re-instated after a public outcry over his sacking?

QUIZ 220

1. Name West Ham's long-serving full-back, whose goal in the 1980 semi-final replay took the Hammers into the FA Cup Final.
2. Tommy Langley was top scorer for which London club in the 1977-78 season?
3. Which top Greek club has a shamrock on its badge?
4. What name did the locals give to Scotland's tough 1986 World Cup Group?
5. Which unusual method of transport did Glasgow bookmaker Jim Tait attempt to hire to take Scotland fans to the 1978 World Cup in Argentina?
6. How many times do teams play each other in the Scottish Second Division?

QUIZ 221

1. In 1955, who scored the quickest-ever Wembley FA Cup Final goal after only 45 seconds of the Manchester City-Newcastle match?
2. Who is the international winger who joined Rangers from Clydebank for £100,000 in 1977?
3. In which year did Manchester United win the European Cup?
4. Name the striker in the 1989 Bournemouth team who notched a hat-trick in England's 9-0 win over Luxembourg in 1982.
5. Which international singing star wrote and sang 'Ole Ola' with the 1978 Scottish World Cup Squad?
6. Which Midlands side defeated Hearts to win the first-ever Texaco Cup in 1971?

QUIZ 222

1. Since the foundation of the Football League, which is the only non-League team to have won the FA Cup?
2. Name the full-back whose clubs include Chelsea, Forest, Portsmouth and Aston Villa with whom he won a European Cup medal in 1982.
3. What is featured on the badge of Red Star Belgrade?
4. For which country did Carlos Caszely appear in the 1974 and 1982 World Cups?
5. Which famous old Everton player died while watching a Merseyside derby in March 1980?
6. The winners of which competition receive the Henri Delaunay Cup?

QUIZ 223

1. In 1953, which Blackpool forward scored an FA Cup Final hat-trick - the last player to do so?
2. Who was the Hibernian wing starlet signed by Arsenal for £100,000 in 1970?
3. What does *Real* mean in Real Madrid's name?
4. Which famous striker scored his last World Cup goal in 1974 - the winner in the Final?
5. Name one of Glasgow's Scottish League clubs, other than Celtic or Rangers.
6. Alex Miller was a long-serving player with which club before turning to management at St Mirren and Hibs?

QUIZ 224

1. Which team did Blackpool defeat in the 'Matthews Final' of 1953?
2. Henry Smith keeps goal for which Scottish club?
3. Which European national team has the letters *KNVB* on its jersey?
4. Who was Argentina's successful 1978 World Cup manager who later took charge at Barcelona?
5. What height was Carlo Nastri, who played for Crystal Palace in the 1958-59 season?
6. What happens if the FA Charity Shield match finishes level after ninety minutes?

QUIZ 225

1. Which team won four consecutive League Cups from 1981 to 1984?
2. Scottish striker Sandy Clark had a spell in London during 1982-83, at which club?
3. Which Soviet midfielder starred for Juventus during 1988-89?
4. Brazil won the 1958 World Cup by beating the host country in the Final - who was this?
5. Top model and singer Samantha Fox is a fan of which London club?
6. Only once has a club been invited into the European Cup which was neither the holders nor the champions of its country - what was the club?

QUIZ 226

1. Which team in 1927 became the only non-English club ever to win the FA Cup?
2. Which was veteran striker Mick Channon's first club?
3. The Parc Astrid in Brussels is home to which club?
4. Which country was eliminated on goal difference in three consecutive World Cups from 1974 to 1982?
5. Which London club plays in a red and blue striped jersey?
6. Which domestic competition was spurned in its early years by many of the top Football League clubs?

QUIZ 227

1. Who was the Manchester City goalkeeper who played for part of the 1956 FA Cup Final with a broken neck?
2. From which club did Everton sign Kevin Sheedy in 1982?
3. The Prater Stadium is the national football ground of which country?
4. Who scored his first-ever goal for Scotland in the 1982 World Cup match against the Soviet Union?
5. Which animal is featured on the badges of Ipswich and Gillingham?
6. Which was the first English competition to use the penalty shoot-out to decide matches?

QUIZ 228

1. How did Arsenal and Sunderland both win the FA Cup in 1979?
2. Mark Lawrenson arrived at Liverpool in 1981, signing for £900,000 from which club?
3. Leeds lost the 1973 Cup-Winners Cup Final - to which Italian side?
4. What is Canada's first choice strip?
5. Why was Michael Robinson unimpressed with the manager who promised to make him an England international within six months?
6. At which club did Terry Yorath begin his management career?

--------------------------- **QUIZ 229** ---------------------------

1. Name the former Dundee, Spurs and Derby striker who became Ipswich manager in 1987.
2. Who is the West Ham full-back and penalty expert who was signed from Dundee United in 1979?
3. What is the name of SV Hamburg's ground?
4. What was the term used to describe the flexible style of Ajax Amsterdam and the Dutch national side in the 1970s?
5. Who is the former Granada football commentator now working for the BBC?
6. What is the reserve league for Southern-based clubs called?

--------------------------- **QUIZ 230** ---------------------------

1. Before Coventry in 1987, which was the last Midlands team to win the FA Cup?
2. For which Lancashire club did Alan Stevenson keep goal in the 1970s?
3. Which is Hungary's national stadium?
4. Who was the Welsh referee who disallowed a Brazilian goal in the 1978 World Cup because he had blown for full-time?
5. What was the title of BBC's theme music for the 1986 World Cup?
6. In the nineteenth century, which term, now associated with cricket, was used for the promotion and relegation play-off games?

--------------------------- **QUIZ 231** ---------------------------

1. For which top club did Gordon West keep goal in the early 1970s?
2. For which team did forward Simon Stainrod play in the 1982 FA Cup Final?
3. Who shot Nottingham Forest's winner in the 1980 European Cup Final against Hamburg?
4. Alan Ball was with which club when he played in the 1966 World Cup?
5. Name the French philosopher-novelist who was also a useful goalkeeper in his native Algeria.
6. Why could Liverpool and Everton not both have competed in the European Fairs Cup competition during the same season?

QUIZ 232

1. Which team won the Centenary FA Cup Final in 1972?
2. The career of which famous goalkeeper was cut short after a Sunday morning car crash cost him the sight of an eye?
3. Which team plays in Lisbon's 'Stadium of Light'?
4. Name the goalkeeper who was captain of Italy's victorious World Cup side of 1982.
5. What is the full name of Scottish club Hearts?
6. Name the Aston Villa star, who in 1977, became the only man to be voted both PFA Player and Young Player of the Year in the same season.

QUIZ 233

1. Name the Leeds player who scored in both matches of the replayed 1970 FA Cup Final.
2. Which three-times European Cup medallist captained Southampton during 1988-89?
3. In which Eastern-bloc country is the 95,000 capacity August 23rd Stadium?
4. What was the significance of Brazil's World Cup win in 1970?
5. Which television presenter once played for Oxford against Cambridge at Wembley?
6. In which country was Ernie Walker the administrative supremo from 1977 to 1989?

QUIZ 234

1. For which team did Neil Young's goal win the 1969 FA Cup?
2. Who was the Reading striker who topped the Third Division goalscoring chart in 1985-86?
3. Which Dutch side ended a run of English success in the Fairs/UEFA Cup by defeating Spurs in the 1974 Final?
4. With which club was Ray Wilkins first capped?
5. Manchester United won the European Cup playing in what colour of strip?
6. What is CONMEBOL?

QUIZ 235

1. Which TV presenter scored the winner in the 1965 FA Cup Final?
2. In 1982, who was the winger, then with QPR, who scored his first senior goal in Northern Ireland's 1-0 win over West Germany?
3. In which Spanish city is the Luis Casanova Stadium?
4. Dave Bowen was once manager of which of the home countries?
5. Name the ex-Leeds and England full-back who made an anti-hooligan record in 1979, with a group of players called 'The Peace Band'.
6. For approximately how long was Mike England Welsh international boss - four, six or eight years?

QUIZ 236

1. Which current manager headed the only goal of the Leeds-Arsenal Cup Final of 1972?
2. In 1982-83, which Leicester forward was the Second Division's top goalscorer?
3. In which country is the Wankdorf Stadium, where the 1989 Cup-Winners Cup Final was held?
4. Who was the unfortunate defender who missed France's last penalty in the shoot-out to decide the 1982 World Cup semi-final?
5. Which team is the football love of Jimmy Tarbuck?
6. Which team did England beat 2-1 at Wembley to mark the Centenary of the Football Association in 1963?

QUIZ 237

1. Who kept goal for Arsenal in the 1972 Centenary FA Cup Final?
2. To which club did Liverpool pay £300,000 for Jan Molby in 1984?
3. Which Juventus star won three consecutive European Footballer of the Year awards from 1983 to 1985?
4. What was the nickname of Peru's madman 1978 World Cup 'keeper Ramon Quiroga?
5. Name the Scottish Second Division team which plays its home matches at Hampden Park.
6. In which round of the Littlewoods Cup do the First Division clubs enter?

QUIZ 238

1. Who was the Arsenal substitute who scored the vital equalizer in the 1971 FA Cup Final with Liverpool?
2. Name the defender who was an accomplished Gaelic footballer with the Pegasus club before turning to soccer with Manchester United in 1978.
3. Which of these stadia has the largest capacity - Bernabeu (Madrid), Lenin (Moscow) or Hampden Park?
4. Which England full-back scored in the 2-0 Wembley victory over Yugoslavia in November 1986?
5. Who was 'transferred' from London Weekend to the BBC in May 1973?
6. Who was the last England manager to be sacked?

QUIZ 239

1. Who headed the goal at White Hart Lane which clinched the League Championship - the first leg of Arsenal's 1971 'Double'?
2. With which Italian club did Jimmy Greaves play?
3. Which Scottish club lost narrowly in the 1967 Cup-Winners Cup Final with Bayern?
4. Which Polish star won his 100th international cap during the 1982 World Cup Tournament?
5. Home Farm play in which league?
6. Englands 1966 World Champion team dispensed with which traditional forward position?

QUIZ 240

1. Who scored the Wembley goal which won the 'Double' for Arsenal in 1971?
2. What are the christian names of the Snodin brothers who played together at Doncaster before moving on to bigger clubs?
3. Which team could you watch in the Stade Geoffroy-Guichard?
4. Which of the two German nations plays in white shirts and blue shorts?
5. Who were once 'The Glaziers' but are now 'The Eagles'?
6. Why does Great Britain not compete in the Olympic Football Tournament?

QUIZ 241

1. Who were the 1989 Fourth Division Champions?
2. Who was the England International winger who played in the First Division for Burnley, QPR and Everton in the 1970s?
3. Which Dutch town is home to FC Twente?
4. In which colour of jersey does Albania's national side play?
5. Name the Glasgow-born midfielder who was sarcastically voted Scottish 'Man of the Match' for the 1987 Scotland-Eire European Championship clash.
6. On the Football Pools, how many points are awarded for an away win?

QUIZ 242

1. Which team reached the FA Cup Final but was also relegated in 1969?
2. With which two clubs did Brian Talbot win FA Cup medals?
3. Which other Italian League club shares the Olimpico Stadium with AS Roma?
4. Who was the powerfully-built Manchester United defender who was Scotland's centre-half in the 1974 World Cup?
5. What are the colours of Leicester City?
6. What office did Graham Kelly hold before becoming Secretary of the FA?

QUIZ 243

1. Who kept goal for Leicester in their 1969 FA Cup Final defeat by Manchester City?
2. Name Spurs twice-capped full-back who was forced to quit the game after sustaining an injury against QPR in March 1987.
3. Name either of the French football teams which play their home matches in the Parc des Princes.
4. How many Scottish caps did Graeme Souness win from 1974 to 1986 - 54, 64 or 74?
5. How many Welsh clubs have played in the First Division?
6. What is the footballing term used to describe the playing of the ball through an opponent's legs?

QUIZ 244

1. In 1975, which then non-League side knocked First Division Burnley out of the FA Cup by winning at Turf Moor?
2. What number of shirt does Liverpool midfielder Ronnie Whelan like to wear?
3. The Bokelberg Stadium is home to which leading West German club?
4. Who was the 17-year-old who played for Northern Ireland in the 1982 World Cup?
5. Which ground have Crystal Palace and Charlton Athletic shared since 1985?
6. In 1986-87, which club considered a merger with Crystal Palace?

QUIZ 245

1. Which team were runners-up in both the Scottish League and Cup in 1985-86?
2. Name the former Oldham and Manchester City defender who is a talented artist.
3. What is the name of Bohemians' Dublin ground which has been occasionally used for internationals?
4. In which country did England enjoy an 8-0 victory while qualifying for the 1986 World Cup?
5. What was the nickname given to Ray Wilkins at Chelsea?
6. The record attendance for a Football League game is for Manchester United's 1948 clash with Arsenal - at which ground?

QUIZ 246

1. With which team did former West Ham skipper Bobby Moore play against the Hammers in an FA Cup Final?
2. Whom do the Liverpool players call 'Wor Pete'?
3. Which club has won the most post-war Austrian League Championships - Rapid Vienna or FK Austria?
4. Who was leading scorer in the Spanish World Cup of 1982?
5. Why was Manchester City full-back Arthur Mann left behind when the team flew to Copenhagen for a European play-off match in 1971?
6. At which leading English club did Martin Edwards succeed his late father Louis as chairman in March 1980?

QUIZ 247

1. Name the West Ham striker whose two goals won the FA Cup in 1975.
2. England striker Tony Woodcock left Arsenal in 1986 to start his second spell at which German club?
3. Which club has won the most Belgian League Championships since the war?
4. Top FIFA referee Paolo Casarin hails from which country?
5. Which top British tennis player of recent years is a fan of Wolves?
6. In which South American country are referees paid 1% of gate receipts?

QUIZ 248

1. Which striker scored two of Liverpool's goals in their 1974 FA Cup triumph over Newcastle?
2. At which club did brothers John and Justin Fashanu both begin their professional careers?
3. Hamburg lifted the 1983 European Cup by defeating which team in the Athens Final?
4. What was it, according to Diego Maradona, that helped him score his first World Cup goal against England in 1986?
5. Which manager co-wrote the TV detective series 'Hazell'?
6. Publisher Robert Maxwell left Oxford in 1987 to become chairman of which First Division club?

QUIZ 249

1. Who hit Sunderland's winning goal in their shock 1973 FA Cup Final victory over Leeds?
2. Name the former Luton striker who joined Spurs in a £500,000 deal in February 1988 after four years at Liverpool.
3. Which has been the most successful German Bundesliga team?
4. Who kept goal for Scotland in the 1986 World Cup?
5. In the 1970s, which Midlands club adopted a change strip of broad green and yellow stripes?
6. Where is the FA's School of Excellence for budding young footballers?

QUIZ 250

1. Name the Sunderland goalkeeper who made a famous Wembley save from Peter Lorimer to help his side lift the 1973 FA Cup.
2. Who is the versatile former England Youth cap whose two goals helped knock Liverpool out of the 1988-89 Littlewoods Cup?
3. Name the Dynamo Kiev striker who was voted European Footballer of the Year in 1986.
4. Which fellow striker did Peter Beardsley replace after two matches in the 1986 World Cup?
5. What is the title of Scottish Television's long-running football and sports programme?
6. In 1987, Howard Kendall left Everton to take charge at which Spanish club?

QUIZ 251

1. Name the striker who was a Wembley loser in 1974 and 1978 with Newcastle and Arsenal respectively.
2. Who succeeded Martin Buchan as Manchester United captain?
3. Which has been the most successful club in Greek football?
4. Walter Zenga was first-choice goalkeeper for which national side in 1988-89?
5. What was the name of the dog which found the World Cup trophy after it had been stolen before the 1966 tournament in England?
6. Name two League clubs which have the letter 'x' in their name.

QUIZ 252

1. Who was the forward who won FA Cup medals with Manchester United in 1977 and West Ham in 1980?
2. What was the surname of twins Ian and Roger who played together at QPR in the 1960s?
3. When Chelsea won the 1971 Cup-Winners Cup, they knocked out the holders - which other British club was this?
4. Against which country did England gain their first victory of the 1986 World Cup Finals?
5. In 1976, which England player was treated in hospital after a cycle crash during the BBC's 'Superstars' competition ?
6. Name two Football League clubs called Athletic.

QUIZ 253

1. Which Welshman captained Southampton to FA Cup glory in 1976?
2. Who was the Everton star of the 1960s known as 'The Golden Vision'?
3. Which club has won the most Italian League titles?
4. Who was the Scottish player, sent home in disgrace from the Argentina World Cup after a positive dope test?
5. Which current top player starred with the 'Two Ronnies' in a TV advertisement for Hertz cars?
6. Who was the Scotland captain who was banned from international football after an incident in a Copenhagen nightclub in 1975?

QUIZ 254

1. Whom did John Lyall succeed as West Ham manager?
2. In January 1988, who became the first black player to appear in the Scottish Premier League?
3. Which has been the dominant club in Portuguese soccer since 1935?
4. Which leading goalscorer never regained his place in England's 1966 World Cup side after being injured in a first round match?
5. What is the official colour of the famous Wolves jersey?
6. What happened to the Wembley goalposts after England's 1977 defeat by Scotland?

QUIZ 255

1. Name Southampton's FA Cup medallist of 1976 who had lost in the Final ten years previously with Sheffield Wednesday.
2. In 1987-88 Ipswich bought back from Liverpool a former midfield star of theirs - who?
3. Which club has captured the most League Championships in Spain?
4. What was the name of Argentina's 1986 World Cup goalkeeper?
5. Which former top manager once took elocution lessons to rid himself of his accent?
6. Which footballing first did Charlton No.12 Keith Peacock achieve at Bolton in August 1965?

QUIZ 256

1. Which striker won FA Cup medals with Chelsea and Southampton during the 1970s?
2. Who is the England international full-back nicknamed 'Spider'?
3. Which has been the all-time most successful Yugoslavian club?
4. Who traditionally contest the opening match in the World Cup Finals?
5. Why did the Colombian Referees Association refuse to provide officials for ladies matches?
6. During his first spell at Liverpool, only one First Division team managed to stop Ian Rush from ever scoring against them - which one?

QUIZ 257

1. Who succeeded Ron Atkinson as West Bromwich Albion manager after only ten games of the 1988-89 season?
2. Who is the Scottish international midfielder who has played for Belgian club Lokeren, Rangers and Aberdeen?
3. Feyenoord hail from which large Dutch port?
4. In the 1982 World Cup, who was the Scotland defender whose 20-yard shot stunned Brazil?
5. Which former Labour Prime Minister once said 'I know more about football than politics'?
6. Which famous Scottish team began life as a rowing club by the Clyde?

QUIZ 258

1. Manchester United's 1977 FA Cup-winning goal was scored by a former Leeds and Stoke City striker. What was his name?
2. Former Sheffield United and Chesterfield goalkeeper Jim Brown was capped by which country in 1975?
3. Which defender fired Liverpool's winner in the 1981 European Cup Final in Paris?
4. Which Central American country plays in green shirts, white shorts and red socks?
5. Where did TV presenter Ian St John begin his professional soccer career?
6. 'Goals for divided by goals against' is a definition of what?

QUIZ 259

1. Jock Wallace, Ian St John and Ally MacLeod have all been manager at which Scottish club?
2. Veteran goalkeeper John Burridge played for which First Division club in 1988-89?
3. In which Belgian city could you watch a derby match between teams called Cercle and Club?
4. Who was the French president of FIFA who was largely responsible for the creation of the World Cup?
5. How does Spanish fan Manolo make a lot of noise at international matches?
6. Is it permissable to remove a corner-flag in order to take a corner-kick?

QUIZ 260

1. Which club appeared in the most FA Cup Finals during the 1970s?
2. Who was the talented Spurs and Scotland inside-forward whose career was tragically cut short in 1964, when he was killed by lightning on a golf-course?
3. Which European capital has teams called Dynamo, Spartak and Torpedo?
4. Who succeeded Alex Ferguson as Scotland boss in 1986?
5. How did the 'Kop' acquire its name?
6. Which personality manager is known as 'Harry'?

QUIZ 261

1. Who scored Ipswich Town's winner in the 1978 Cup Final and then had to be substituted through exhaustion?
2. John Chiedozie, who has played for Orient, Notts County, Spurs and Derby, is a full international for which country?
3. Which Belgian town boasts a famous team called Standard?
4. In Wales-Ireland internationals, which country has won the more games?
5. What was the title of the record made by the England World Cup squad of 1982?
6. Where was the League Cup Final played prior to 1967?

QUIZ 262

1. Which current Second Division manager skippered Ipswich to FA Cup success in 1978?
2. Who is the Northern Ireland international dubbed 'Russ' by his teammates at Manchester United because of his likeness to comedian Russ Abbott?
3. In which country does RWD Molenbeek play?
4. Goalkeeper Mazurkiewicz starred for which country in the 1970 World Cup?
5. Which of the Sheffield clubs is nicknamed 'The Blades'?
6. How many different goalkeepers did Partick Thistle use in the 1987-88 Scottish League season?

QUIZ 263

1. From 1924 to 1926, a Yorkshire club won three consecutive League Championships - which club?
2. Name the Stoke goalkeeper who threatened to quit football in 1982 after being sent off for handling outside his area.
3. Which top Bulgarian side was disbanded after a riot in the 1985 Cup Final, but reformed under the name of Sredets?
4. Northern Ireland boss Billy Bingham has played for his country in the World Cup - in which year?
5. Why are Southampton known as 'The Saints'?
6. Which Football League club has the longest name?

QUIZ 264

1. Who scored Millwall's first-ever Division One goal in the match against Aston Villa in August 1988?
2. Who was the tough-tackling Chelsea defender known as 'Chopper'?
3. Which German side has eliminated Rangers from European competition on three occasions since 1979?
4. Against which South American country did England play a dour goalless draw in the opening match of the 1966 World Cup?
5. Who are 'The Cumbrians'?
6. Allan Harris has been the long-standing assistant to which top manager?

QUIZ 265

1. What is the furthest that a Fourth Division club has progressed in the FA Cup?
2. Which former Scotland boss played in the 1960 FA Cup Final for Blackburn Rovers?
3. Which Liverpool player received his marching orders in the 1982 European Cup quarter-final in Sofia?
4. Who is the goalkeeper who is the tallest man ever to have played for England?
5. What is featured on Arsenal's shirt badge?
6. What should be given if a defender inadvertently strikes a direct free-kick back into his own net?

QUIZ 266

1. How many English-born players lined up for Liverpool in the 1986 FA Cup Final against Everton?
2. Who are the twins who have played together at Chester, Luton, Manchester City and Barnsley?
3. Banik Ostrava play in which country?
4. The 1000th goal in World Cup Final tournaments was scored by Holland's Robbie Resenbrink in 1978 - against which of the British nations?
5. Which common colour of goalkeeping jersey were Football League goalkeepers not permitted to wear until the mid-1980s?
6. In which round of the FA Cup do First and Second Division clubs enter?

QUIZ 267

1. Which club beat Hyde United 26-0 in the FA Cup in October 1887?
2. Who was the only Evertonian in Scotland's 1986 World Cup squad?
3. Name the Borussia Moenchengladbach striker who hit two goals in the 1973 UEFA Cup Final against Liverpool.
4. Which country eliminated Brazil in a penalty shoot-out in the 1986 World Cup?
5. Which Scottish team plays at Easter Road?
6. Who won the rematch of the 1966 World Cup Final, played in Leeds in 1985 for the Bradford fire disaster fund?

QUIZ 268

1. With which team did leading manager Terry Venables win a League Cup winners medal in 1965?
2. Who was the English-born goalkeeper who helped Celtic win the Scottish League in 1977 and 1979?
3. Brondby competed in this season's European Cup as representatives of which country?
4. Austrian Ernst Happel managed which country in the 1978 World Cup?
5. For which Football League club has England cricket star Ian Botham played?
6. Name the former Liverpool striker who became manager of Spanish giants Real Madrid during 1989.

QUIZ 269

1. Which striker scored FA Cup Final goals for Arsenal in 1979 and Manchester United in 1983?
2. At 16 years and 57 days, Jason Dozzell became the youngest-ever First Division scorer in 1984 - for which club did he net?
3. Which Soviet team convincingly defeated Atletico Madrid 3-0 to take the 1986 Cup-Winners Cup?
4. Which unfancied side led Portugal by 3-0 in the 1966 World Cup quarter-final before eventually losing 5-3?
5. Which regional ITV company broadcast a football magazine programme called 'Kick Off'?
6. Where was George Graham's first managerial appointment?

QUIZ 270

1. Which team did Arsenal take four games to beat in the 1980 FA Cup semi-final?
2. With which club did Ian Bowyer win a European Cup-Winners Cup medal in 1970?
3. On which Mediterranean island could you watch France's 1978 UEFA Cup Finalists Bastia play?
4. According to England boss Ron Greenwood, whose name was always first on his teamsheet?
5. In which English city do both the League clubs play in striped shirts?
6. Which club has won the League Championship more often - Blackburn Rovers or Bolton Wanderers?

QUIZ 271

1. Who scored for Everton in the 1980 FA Cup semi-final with West Ham before being sent off in the second half?
2. For which country was Dick Krzywicki an international?
3. Which East German side is called after a famous optical works?
4. Where did Wales play Scotland in their 1977 World Cup qualifying section decider?
5. In which colour of jersey do Hearts play?
6. The world record attandance for a club match is for the Fluminese-Flamengo derby of 1963 - in which city?

QUIZ 272

1. Recently playing in the lower divisions of the League, this club was generally regarded as having English Football's 'Team of the Fifties' - which club?
2. What was the name of Bobby and Jack Charlton's uncle who scored 178 League goals for Newcastle between 1946 and 1957?
3. Which top Greek club plays in the port of Piraeus?
4. Who was Scotland's manager in the 1982 World Cup Finals?
5. Pop stars Craig and Charlie Reid of 'The Proclaimers' both follow which team?
6. Who is the former Liverpool full-back who became manager of Bolton in 1985?

QUIZ 273

1. Which was the last Second Division club to win the FA Cup?
2. Which striker did Rangers sign from Atalanta in 1987?
3. Which Welsh club has made the most appearances in European competition?
4. In the 1982 World Cup, which country qualified from the Second Phase at the expense of England?
5. What is the name of the popular end of Manchester United's Old Trafford ground, where their vociferous home support congregates?
6. Former Newcastle boss Willie McFaul was an international goalkeeper for which country?

QUIZ 274

1. Which England star headed West Ham's 1980 FA Cup-winning goal?
2. Which Manchester United defender missed out on their 1977 FA Cup win after breaking his leg two weeks before the Final?
3. Who scored the penalty for Juventus which beat Liverpool in the tragedy-hit 1985 European Cup Final in Brussels?
4. Who was the Brazilian World Cup star turned down by Irish club Shelbourne while he was a medical student in Dublin?
5. What is featured on the badge of Nottingham Forest?
6. Who was the former Football League secretary and orginator of the League Cup competition who died in 1980?

QUIZ 275

1. Which of the Edinburgh teams did Celtic trounce 6-1 in the 1972 Scottish Cup Final?
2. Who was the Rangers, Hearts and WBA winger who was sent off fifteen times in his career?
3. In which country does the Valur club play?
4. Which player played in the 1954 World Cup for Hungary but turned out for Spain in the 1962 tournament?
5. Name the flamboyant millionaire racehourse owner who became chairman of Walsall in 1986.
6. During the British summer, football pools companies use the fixtures of which other country?

QUIZ 276

1. Which team did Spurs beat in a replay to win their first FA Cup of the 1980s.
2. Can you name the former Dundee captain forced to quit football after being injured during a match at Ibrox in September 1987?
3. What is the name of the Italian League side from Florence?
4. Northern Ireland scored five goals during the 1982 World Cup Tournament. Gerry Armstrong scored three - which player scored the other two?
5. In which colour of shirts did Arsenal contest the 1978, 1979 and 1980 FA Cup Finals?
6. Name either of the sides which Herbert Chapman managed to League Championship success.

QUIZ 277

1. Why did Tottenham's Ricky Villa miss the 1982 FA Cup Final?
2. Who was, surprisingly, Manchester United's leading goalscorer at one stage of the 1973-74 season?
3. Which striker scored for Chelsea in the 1971 Cup-Winners Cup Final and also in the replay?
4. What are the first-choice colours of Uruguay?
5. Which club plays at Bootham Crescent?
6. What was the name of Tampa Bay's NASL team who said that soccer was 'A Kick in the Grass'?

QUIZ 278

1. Which Spurs player was tripped by Tony Currie to earn the vital penalty which settled the 1982 FA Cup Final Replay?
2. Name the full-back who played in the 1975 and 1980 European Cup Finals - with different clubs.
3. Jeunesse d'Esch are the all-time most successful club in which small European country?
4. In which colour of strip does Holland play?
5. Name the Scottish League club whose ground is in England.
6. Which annual fixture was switched to Wembley in 1974?

QUIZ 279

1. Which seaside club, Fourth Division Champions in 1973, had lost its League status by 1978?
2. Name the Welshman who has played for both Barcelona and Bayern Munich in recent seasons.
3. In which country does the team called Hibernians play?
4. Which nation won the *Mundialito*, the mini-World Cup for past winners, in January 1981?
5. Which manager was known as 'Snoz' during his playing days?
6. What is the name of Diego Maradona's younger brother who, in 1987, was also signed by Napoli before being farmed out on loan to Ascoli?

QUIZ 280
---

1. Which fellow London club did Spurs beat in the 1982 FA Cup Final?
2. Name one of the clubs of international midfielder Alan Hudson.
3. Which is the only club to have won all three major European tournaments?
4. Who was Scotland's manager in the 1974 World Cup Finals in West Germany?
5. Which two British teams are nicknamed 'The Dons'?
6. What is the leading knock-out competition for non-League clubs?

QUIZ 281
---

1. Lou Macari scored in the 1971 Scottish Cup Final replay - for which club?
2. Who was the Swindon superstar who joined Crystal Palace for £150,000 in October 1972?
3. From which Dutch town does AZ 67 hail?
4. The entire Scotland team for the 1872 international with England was supplied by which famous amateur club?
5. What was the title of the official film of the 1966 World Cup?
6. The 'Sounders' were based in which American city?

QUIZ 282
---

1. Which Midlands team lost in FA Cup semi-finals in 1978 and 1982, both played at Highbury?
2. Gary Sprake, Leeds 'keeper of the Don Revie era, was an international for which country?
3. Which was the first English team to compete in the European Cup?
4. Who was the Brazilian, ordered off during the crunch 1974 World Cup match with Holland in Dortmund?
5. Which footballer's autobiography is entitled *No Half Measures*?
6. Name the Scottish striker who played for the Italian League against the Scottish League in 1961.

QUIZ 283

1. Ricky Villa scored two of Spurs' goals when they beat Manchester City 3-2 to win the 1981 FA Cup. Which striker, recently with Charlton, scored the other goal?
2. Which Italian club signed Mark Hateley and Ray Wilkins in 1984?
3. What is the forward-thinking name of the Dutch League club from Deventer?
4. Who won the 1950 World Cup Final?
5. Bramall Lane, home of Sheffield United, was formerly used for which sport as well as football?
6. In 1984, how did Bristol City decide whether Howard Pritchard or Alan Crawford had scored for them against Wrexham?

QUIZ 284

1. In 1983, which team chalked up the biggest-ever Wembley FA Cup Final victory?
2. Who was the Everton player, signed from Luton, who hit a memorable winning goal in the Merseyside derby of October 1978?
3. Which Spurs player scored an own-goal in the first leg and was sent off in the second leg of a 1985 UEFA Cup tie with Real Madrid?
4. In what colour of jersey does Iceland play by choice?
5. For which soccer magazine does Jimmy Greaves write the letters column?
6. Which club defeated Forest 2-1 in ITV's first-ever live Football League game in October 1983?

QUIZ 285

1. Name the manager who took Brighton to Wembley in 1983.
2. Who was the Wolves star who walked out on the club in 1969 to become a Jehovah's Witness?
3. In which country do the clubs Lillestrom and Fredrikstad play?
4. Who scored the two goals which gave Scotland a crucial World Cup victory over France in March 1989?
5. What is the name of the former manager's secretary, now Roy's wife in *Roy of the Rovers*?
6. What happened to League players who deliberately handled during the 1982-83 season?

QUIZ 286

1. Which feat has been achieved by Roger Hunt, Tony Brown and Luther Blissett?
2. Grey-haired Alan Woodward played over 500 games for which Yorkshire club?
3. Which team defeated Dundee United on aggregate to take the 1987 UEFA Cup?
4. Name the manager who steered Italy to victory in the 1982 World Cup.
5. Which former England captain married Joy Beverley of the singing Beverley Sisters?
6. Which Manchester team has won the FA Cup more often - United or City?

QUIZ 287

1. In 1983, which team lost to Manchester United in both the Milk Cup and FA Cup semi-finals?
2. What was the nickname of Carlisle, Newcastle, Sunderland and West Ham striker Bryan Robson?
3. In which European city are the headquarters of UEFA?
4. Who was the first player to score against England in the 1966 World Cup tournament?
5. What are the three colours of Glasgow Rangers?
6. Which top star won a car by being named Man of the Match when Flamengo beat Liverpool 3-0 in the 1981 World Club Championship in Tokyo?

QUIZ 288

1. Which Scottish striker missed a great chance for Brighton in the dying minutes of the drawn 1983 FA Cup Final with Manchester United?
2. Who was known as the 'Wizard of Dribble'?
3. Lech Poznan and Stal Mielec play in which European country?
4. Name the Scotland winger who had to be rescued at sea after being lost in a rowing boat during preparation for the match against England in 1974.
5. Name the popular table-soccer game where player figures are 'flicked to kick'.
6. What fundamental change in the throw-in law was introduced in 1987?

QUIZ 289

1. Peter Noble netted 29 consecutive penalties from 1974 to 1979. With which club was he playing?
2. Liverpool defender Alan Kennedy left Anfield in 1985 to join which Second Division club?
3. Which Polish town has teams called Widzew and LKS?
4. For which country has Joel Bats kept goal since 1983?
5. What is the name of West Bromwich Albion's ground?
6. What was the attendance at the 1979 Meadowbank-Stenhousemuir clash - 80, 180 or 280?

QUIZ 290

1. Which internationalist, later to join Spurs, scored a late equalizer for Brighton in the 1983 FA Cup Final against Manchester United?
2. Who was the Welshman who won a European Cup medal with Liverpool in 1977?
3. Of which Portuguese club was ex-Spurs boss Keith Burkinshaw manager from January 1987 to February 1988?
4. How many England caps did midfielder Terry McDermott win - 5, 15 or 25?
5. Which Scottish team are nicknamed 'The Hibees' by their fans?
6. Name the striker, then with West Ham, who was voted Young Player of the Year for 1985-86.

QUIZ 291

1. Which club did Tony Waddington manage from 1960 to 1977?
2. Tommy Lawton was a top scorer in the 1930s and 40s. Can you name any two of his six League clubs?
3. Which Portuguese side did Manchester United defeat to win the European Cup in 1968?
4. In which year did midfielder Paul McStay make his Scotland debut - 1981, 1983 or 1985?
5. Which team did Kenny Dalglish support as a boy?
6. If a team wins the UEFA Cup, how many games will it have played in the competition?

QUIZ 292

1. Which team made its first Wembley appearance in 1984, losing 2-0 to Everton?
2. Which striker moved from Barcelona to Hibs in the summer of 1988?
3. In which country would you watch Dynamo Zagreb play Vardar Skopje?
4. Who holds the record for the most consecutive appearances for England - 70 in all?
5. What is the nickname of Spanish World Cup striker Emilio Butragueno?
6. What does it mean if a player is 'cup-tied'?

QUIZ 293

1. Which was the last Third Division club to reach the FA Cup semi-finals?
2. Kevin Lock won an FA Cup medal in 1975 - with which club?
3. What number did Johan Cruyff always like to wear for Ajax and Holland?
4. Which member of the 1978 Argentinian World Cup team sampled English League football with Birminghan City?
5. Two members of Scotland's 1982 World Cup squad had surnames which were names of countries - name either?
6. Before the penalty shoot-out was introduced, what was used as a tie-break in European competitions?

QUIZ 294

1. Which team knocked Liverpool out of the FA Cup in successive seasons from 1983 to 1984?
2. Which First Division side did Les Briley captain during 1988-89?
3. University Craiova plays in which country?
4. Who scored the vital penalty equalizer for Scotland in their crunch World Cup qualifying tie with Wales in September 1985?
5. In the 1970s, which First Division side wore a change strip of black and green stripes?
6. Between 1930 and 1986, how many times was the World Cup won by the host nation?

QUIZ 295

1. Holders Manchester United crashed out of the 1984 FA Cup at which Third Division club?
2. Who succeeded Emlyn Hughes as captain of Liverpool?
3. Which Welsh non-League team lost only 1-0 to Atletico in a 1985 Cup-Winners Cup match in Madrid?
4. In what way was Brazilian winger Jairzinho consistent during the 1970 World Cup?
5. Which anthropologist wrote *The Soccer Tribe* - a book which compares football to primeval tribalism?
6. What did the Northern Premier League become in 1985?

QUIZ 296

1. Which non-League side eliminated four League clubs before going out to holders Everton in the 1985 FA Cup?
2. What is the surname of brothers Tom and Colin who opposed each other in a Celtic-Rangers match in 1980?
3. Who are Barcelona's city neighbours - the 1988 UEFA Cup runners-up?
4. Which European national team are known as 'Les Diables Rouges' (Red Devils)?
5. Which top English club was the first to introduce private boxes in its ground?
6. In the summer of 1988, which Football League club made history by appointing a Uruguayan manager?

QUIZ 297

1. Which Third Division side produced the shock of the 1984-85 season when a late Keith Houchen penalty knocked Arsenal out of the FA Cup?
2. Who was the winger signed by Tommy Docherty at Manchester United, Derby and QPR?
3. In which Spanish town does Athletico Osasuna play?
4. Who captained Northern Ireland's shock troops in the 1982 World Cup?
5. What was the nickname of economics graduate Alan Gowling at Manchester United?
6. Have Spurs won the FA Cup more often than Arsenal?

---------------------------- **QUIZ 298** ----------------------------

1. Which celebrity manager of recent years skippered Oxford United from the Southern League in 1962 to the Third Division Title in 1968?
2. In which country was striker Niall Quinn born?
3. Majorca's leading Spanish League team is called what?
4. Who was the balding Polish striker who was leading scorer in the 1974 World Cup?
5. In 1987, which Everton star dyed his grey hair black?
6. Which Scottish team used to be called Dundee Hibernians?

---------------------------- **QUIZ 299** ----------------------------

1. Name the Manchester United defender who, in 1985, became the first player ever to be sent off in an FA Cup Final.
2. Which Scottish defender, now a manager, was known as 'Caesar' in his playing days?
3. Which two British clubs met in the first round of the 1988-89 European Cup-Winners Cup?
4. Which country eliminated Scotland from the 1982 World Cup by holding them to a 2-2 draw?
5. Who is the Rangers player who was born in Stockholm?
6. Who was the Celtic centre-half voted the first-ever Scottish Footballer of the Year in 1965?

---------------------------- **QUIZ 300** ----------------------------

1. Who curled a left-foot shot past Everton's Neville Southall to win the 1985 FA Cup for Manchester United?
2. With which club did Steve Powell win a League Championship medal in the 1970s?
3. In which Basque town does Spanish side Real Sociedad play?
4. Who was the English referee who awarded a penalty to Holland in the first minute of the 1974 World Cup Final?
5. What does Crystal Palace goalkeeper Perry Suckling keep in his net for good luck?
6. In 1983, which Liverpool star received both the Footballer of the Year and the PFA Player of the Year awards?

──────────── **QUIZ 301** ────────────

1. Which club's former managers include John Hart, John Benson and Ron Saunders?
2. Which flame-haired Scottish international striker joined Nottingham Forest from Coventry for £1.25 million in 1980?
3. If you were watching a league match between Osters Vaxjo and Djurgardens, in which Scandanavian country would you be?
4. Who captained the 1974 West German World Cup-winning team?
5. What are the colours of Walsall?
6. A foul has been committed but the referee's decision is that to stop play would be unbeneficial to the offended team. What is this called?

──────────── **QUIZ 302** ────────────

1. Which British team won every tournament which it entered in the 1966-67 season?
2. Who is the former Orient and QPR defender who joined Watford in June 1989, after six seasons at Newcastle?
3. Who was the Ipswich striker who scored seven European Cup preliminary round goals against Floriana of Malta in 1962?
4. Josef Masopust notched a goal in the 1962 World Cup Final - for which European country was he playing?
5. Which side did Alf Ramsey brand as 'Animals' in 1966?
6. In the Laws of the Game, there are two kicks which must be played forward. Name either.

──────────── **QUIZ 303** ────────────

1. Which Celtic striker was sensationally ordered off during the 1986-87 Skol Cup Final at Hampden?
2. Calcutta-born Kevin Keelan was a goalkeeper with which club in the 1970s?
3. Which Portuguese star was nicknamed the 'Black Panther' because of his electrifying pace?
4. Who won the 1955-56 Home International Championship?
5. Who was the Sunderland striker who was assualted by a Chelsea fan after helping to knock his old club out of the 1985 Milk Cup at Stamford Bridge?
6. In a football ground, what is the standing area in front of the grandstand usually called?

QUIZ 304

1. What have recent Barnsley managers Norman Hunter, Bobby Collins and Allan Clarke in common?
2. Name one non-English club for which Joe Jordan played.
3. By what youthful-sounding name are Switzerland's 1987 Cup-winners known?
4. Arsenal's Alex James was an international for which country?
5. Which First Division ground has a Bridgford End and a Trent End?
6. Who is the television pundit and former Partick Thistle manager who was voted the 1978 Scottish Footballer of the Year while playing for Rangers?

QUIZ 305

1. Which Southampton player suffered a broken leg in the 1986 FA Cup semi-final with Liverpool?
2. Who became Britain's first £200,000 player when he left West Ham for Spurs in March 1970?
3. Which Italian club paid £2½ million to Flamengo for Brazilian star Zico in 1983?
4. In 1977, which country achieved its first-ever Wembley victory - in its thirteenth match at the stadium?
5. What put TV coverage of the 1969 FA Cup Final in jeopardy for a while?
6. Has a Third Division side ever won the FA Cup?

QUIZ 306

1. Which team reached three consecutive FA Cup Finals during the 1980s?
2. Name the former Manchester United and Eire goalkeeper who played for Halifax from 1984 to 1989.
3. Ex-Spurs and England striker Martin Chivers also played in which country with FC Servette?
4. Which European country took third place in the 1974 and 1982 World Cup Tournaments?
5. Which Ulster club plays in the League of Ireland at a ground called Brandywell?
6. What is the maximum number of substitutes allowed in a friendly match?

QUIZ 307

1. In 1986, against which team did Gary Lineker score his last goal for Everton before leaving for Barcelona?
2. What is the surname of brothers Raymond, Rodney and Danny - who all played in the 1988-89 Southampton team?
3. Which European city does the team called Grasshoppers spring from?
4. Who was the Northern Ireland star ordered off against Scotland in 1970, for throwing mud at the referee?
5. Which London side play in red jerseys at a ground called Brisbane Road?
6. Who was Leeds manager when they dropped into Division Two in 1982?

QUIZ 308

1. Which Liverpool player hit a double in the 1986 FA Cup Final with neighbours Everton?
2. In the 1960s, which team had the all-Irish full-back partnership of Brennan and Dunne?
3. Galatasary play in which Turkish city?
4. Which country beat England 2-1 in a 1981 World Cup qualifying match to the delight of their commentator who lapsed into a monologue about English history?
5. Singer Rod Stewart is an avid fan of which of the British national teams?
6. Have City or Rovers won the more matches in Bristol derbies?

QUIZ 309

1. Besides Liverpool and Everton, which were the last two teams from the same city to contest the FA Cup Final?
2. What is the first name of Mark Hateley's father who played for Notts County, Coventry and many other clubs?
3. Name the Soviet Union's star goalkeeper who joined Seville from Moscow Spartak in December 1988.
4. Which 'minnow' country did Scotland beat 5-2 in the 1982 World Cup in Spain?
5. Which team did Small Heath become?
6. Which club appeared in fourteen consecutive Scottish League Cup Finals from 1964 to 1978?

QUIZ 310

1. In 1985, which member of the FA Cup-winning team did not receive a medal after the match?
2. Who was the only Liverpool player in Scotland's 1986 World Cup squad?
3. Which Manchester United striker missed their European Cup Final victory through injury?
4. Who was the Brazilian nicknamed 'Little Bird' who starred in three World Cups?
5. In 1968-69, what did Coventry's Willie Carr do at a free-kick which has since been declared illegal?
6. Who won the 1985 and 1987 Bell's Manager of the Year awards?

QUIZ 311

1. Did Kenny Dalglish play for Liverpool in the 1986 FA Cup Final against Everton?
2. Which Blackpool striker scored the 1974-75 'Goal of the Season' with a great solo effort against Sunderland?
3. Which entire club side was used as the Soviet national team in 1975-76?
4. Which 1986 World Cup team was called 'Red and White Dynamite' by its fans?
5. How long after kick-off was Jim Fryatt's goal for Bradford against Tranmere in 1964?
6. What did Graham Moore do while at Cardiff, Chelsea, Manchester United, Northampton and Charlton?

QUIZ 312

1. Which Liverpool player missed the 1986 FA Cup Final because of a stomach bug?
2. Which international striker kept goal for Coventry in the 1988 Guinness Soccer Six tournament in Manchester?
3. From which major Soviet city does the club sponsored by camera-makers Zenit come?
4. Which England star was accused of stealing a bracelet in Colombia during the 1970 World Cup build-up?
5. In 1965, who played his last match for Stoke City at the age of 50?
6. If a player leans on a team-mate to gain height for a header, should the referee take any action?

QUIZ 313

1. Which of these clubs has won the FA Trophy most often - Altrincham, Barnet or Scarborough?
2. In which team's defence did converted midfielder Terry Wilson star during 1988-89?
3. Former Rangers general manager Willie Waddell is credited with originating which annual European event in 1973?
4. Manuel Negrete scored with an acrobatic scissors-kick against Bulgaria in the 1986 World Cup - for which country was he playing?
5. Who plays at Leeds Road?
6. Which photographic company were the first sponsors of the Football League?

QUIZ 314

1. Which team won the first Freight Rover Trophy in 1985?
2. Who was the balding 1960s striker who played for Burnley, Leicester and later Aston Villa?
3. Which Italian club is backed by the Agnelli family, directors of the Fiat Motor Enterprise?
4. Both of Scotland's goalscorers in the 1974 World Cup played for the same English club - which one?
5. What are the colours of Luton Town?
6. What was different about the ties in the 1945-46 FA Cup?

QUIZ 315

1. Which team thrashed Ipswich 5-0 in the 1978 Charity Shield match?
2. Which Scottish player walked out on Spurs in 1970 because of homesickness?
3. What is *Bayern* in the club name FC Bayern Munich?
4. Who was the French player whose neck was broken by a vicious challenge from German goalkeeper Schumacher in a 1982 World Cup game?
5. Which team does 'Minder' star Dennis Waterman follow?
6. Which two neighbouring European countries applied to FIFA to jointly host the 1990 World Cup?

QUIZ 316

1. Which team defeated Manchester City 5-4 in the thrilling 1986 Full Members Cup Final at Wembley?
2. Welsh international Pat Van den Hauwe was actually born in which country?
3. What is the significance of the '04' in the name of Schalke 04?
4. How many times have Argentina won the World Cup?
5. In the 1970s, which club used a hot-air balloon as an anti-frost measure?
6. Which Scotland manager also bossed Hearts and Hibernian?

QUIZ 317

1. Which Liverpool player put through his own goal to let Everton win the 1984 Charity Shield match?
2. Which Yorkshire club did Phil Thompson join in 1984, after 14 years at Liverpool?
3. Which midfielder missed a vital kick for Arsenal in the penalty decider of the 1980 Cup-Winners Cup Final with Valencia?
4. Who was the midfielder in France's 1986 World Cup side who was actually born in Spain?
5. Why were Ghana suspended from all FIFA competitions in 1987?
6. Which English club signed Francisco Ernani Lima da Silva in August 1987?

QUIZ 318

1. Who was the 18-year old who came in as replacement for Peter Shilton in Nottingham Forest's victorious 1978 League Cup Final side?
2. At which club did winger Clive Walker begin his League career?
3. The Pirelli tyre company has traditionally given backing to which of the Milan clubs?
4. In which style of jersey does Paraguay play?
5. Meadow Lane is the home of which club?
6. By what other name is the Toyota Cup known?

QUIZ 319

1. Which team won all its games in the 1898-99 Scottish First Division?
2. Name the former Swansea player-manager who scored a hat-trick for Wales against Scotland at Cardiff in 1979.
3. What is *Dozsa* in the name of the Hungarian side Ujpest Dozsa?
4. Name the striker, then with Manchester City, who scored two of England's goals in the 1982 World Cup Finals.
5. By what name is the Empire Stadium better known?
6. During the early years of League football, in what way was the off-side law different from today?

QUIZ 320

1. Which club won the first Scottish 'Treble' in 1949?
2. Name the Welsh winger who played in Division One for Manchester United, Everton, Brighton, Stoke and Chelsea.
3. What is the full name of the club commonly known as Inter-Milan?
4. Which Eastern European nation has played 16 games in the final stages of the World Cup without a single victory?
5. Which team went unbeaten in 85 home League games from 1978 to 1981?
6. Which American-style feature was added to Scotland's strip in 1980?

QUIZ 321

1. Hearts record defeat of 7-0 was inflicted in 1973 - by which team?
2. Which midfielder joined Liverpool from Home Farm in 1979?
3. Which Czech side from Ostrava ended Dundee United's European aspirations in 1987-88?
4. Who was the succesful West German manager in the 1974 World Cup?
5. In 1969, which top Scottish side changed from an all-white strip to a tangerine and black outfit?
6. Which 1989-90 Fourth Division club has competed in the European Cup?

QUIZ 322

1. Which club has won the most Scottish Premier Division Championships since its inception in 1975?
2. Which Irishman, in 1983, became the youngest player ever to score in the FA Cup Final?
3. In which country does the team called Rabat Ajax play?
4. Name the Juventus midfielder who scored Italy's vital second goal in the 1982 World Cup Final with a raging shot.
5. Which team was called Abbey United until 1949?
6. What was remarkable about all twelve of Uruguay's First Division clubs in the 1978-79 season?

QUIZ 323

1. Who were the first ever winners of the Scottish League?
2. Which of England's World Cup winning side was also a first-class cricketer with Essex?
3. Hajduk Split represented which country in the 1987-88 Cup-Winners Cup?
4. Which country eliminated holders Brazil from the 1974 World Cup?
5. Why are Sheffield Wednesday nicknamed 'The Owls'?
6. Have West Ham ever been League Champions?

QUIZ 324

1. Which club won nine consecutive Scottish League Championships from 1966 to 1974?
2. With which club did England goalkeeper Chris Woods make his Football League debut in 1979?
3. Which common feature links Honved, Steaua Bucharest and Dukla Prague?
4. Which of these top managers never won a full international cap as a player - Brian Clough, George Graham or Howard Kendall?
5. What are the colours of Argentinian club Boca Juniors?
6. What was created at an informal meeting at Anderton's Hotel, London in 1888?

QUIZ 325

1. Who are the only post-war Scottish League Champions not currently playing in the Premier League?
2. For which team was Trevor Whymark a top goalscorer in the 1970s?
3. Spanish Second Division side Castilla are the nursery team of which major club?
4. Which League had the more representatives in Scotland's 1986 World Cup squad - the Scottish Premier or the Football League First Division?
5. Which impressionist once had a trial with Oldham but was told he was 'too skinny'?
6. Has any team ever held the FA Cup for more than three years?

QUIZ 326

1. Name the manager of Celtic's great side of the late 1960s and early 70s.
2. With which major club did Scottish international winger Willie Morgan make his name?
3. At which Spanish club did World Cup stars Bonhof and Kempes play together?
4. Which Chelsea signing of 1988 took part in the Seoul Olympic Games?
5. Which English club ground has the same name as a famous golf-course?
6. How wide is a football goal?

QUIZ 327

1. Gerry Daly was top League goalscorer at which club in the 1978-79 season?
2. Colin Viljoen of Ipswich was an international for which country?
3. Which Irish star played in the Juventus-Porto Cup-Winners Cup Final of 1984?
4. What was the surname of Italians Valentino and his son Sandrino who were both stars for Italy's national side?
5. Which club replaced its controversial Omniturf pitch with grass in 1988?
6. Which country drew 1-1 with Portugal in a World Cup qualifying match at Highfield Road, Coventry in March 1973?

QUIZ 328

1. Who were the beaten semi-finalists in the 1989 FA Cup?
2. For which Second Division club did Kevin Keegan sign immediately after the 1982 World Cup?
3. In which German city could you watch the teams Hertha and Blau-Weiss?
4. Who handled the ball when Scotland were awarded a vital penalty in the World Cup qualifier with Wales in October 1977?
5. In 1971, what did Halifax want to do to augment the noise of their crowd?
6. Gary Pendrey resigned as manager of which club in April 1989?

QUIZ 329

1. What was the nickname of the Celtic side which defeated Inter-Milan in Lisbon to lift the 1967 European Cup?
2. Who was the Everton defender with the famous footballing name who joined Birmingham in 1983?
3. The *Oberliga* is the top division of which European country?
4. Which South American country won the 1987 Rous Cup?
5. Which Spurs star was the youngest-ever FA Cup Finalist when he appeared for West Ham in 1980?
6. If a player shouts 'OK, my ball!' as he attempts to collect a ball, should the referee take any action?

QUIZ 330

1. Name the current manager whose headed goal won the 1976 Scottish League Cup for Rangers.
2. Which member of Chelsea's 1970 FA Cup winning-side was tragically killed in a car-crash in March 1977?
3. Which major European country's top league is called the *Serie 'A'*?
4. At which Merseyside ground did the epic Portugal-North Korea 1966 World Cup match take place?
5. Brentford play in striped jerseys - of which colours?
6. South America's 1987 club champions Penarol hail from which country?

QUIZ 331

1. Which manager guided Aberdeen to European success in 1983?
2. With 31 League and Cup goals, Tommy Tynan was the Football League's leading goalscorer in 1982-83 - which club was he then with?
3. Which Austrian club did Everton defeat in Rotterdam to lift the 1985 Cup-Winners Cup?
4. Northern Ireland boss Billy Bingham once managed which other national side?
5. What are the colours of Wigan Athletic?
6. Who is the only man to have captained winning sides in both World Cup and European Cup Finals?

QUIZ 332

1. Howard Kendall played in two losing FA Cup Final sides - one was Everton, what was the other?
2. Who is the Scottish international whose 1971 transfer from West Bromwich to Leeds fell through when a heart defect was discovered during his medical?
3. Name the two Italian clubs which share Turin's 71,000 capacity Stadio Comunale.
4. Why was Haitian Ernst Jean-Joseph barred from further participation in the 1974 World Cup?
5. Which club plays its home matches at Fratton Park?
6. Whose record of 43 goals in a season for Spurs was beaten by Clive Allen in 1987?

QUIZ 333

1. In 1985-86, which team put together a 27-game unbeaten run only to lose the Scottish Premier Championship on the last day of the season?
2. Kenny Hibbitt played most of his career at which club?
3. Which country defeated West Germany on penalties to win the 1976 European Championships?
4. How many players did Scotland take to the 1954 World Cup in Switzerland?
5. Which 'James Bond' once played for East Fife?
6. What has Italian Vittorio Pozzo achieved that is unique in international football management?

QUIZ 334

1. Has the FA Cup gone to Merseyside more often than Manchester?
2. For which club did Iain McCulloch score 16 First Division goals in 1981-82?
3. Which country hosted the final stages of the 1976 European Championships - themselves finishing fourth?
4. In late 1988, which country notched World Cup victories over both Eire and Northern Ireland in the space of five weeks?
5. Which League of Ireland club plays in a similar strip to Celtic?
6. Which First Division club defeated the French national side in a February 1989 friendly?

QUIZ 335

1. Which team, despite being reduced to ten men, defeated Rangers 4-2 to win the Scottish League Title decider of 1979?
2. For which country was inside-forward Ivor Allchurch capped 68 times?
3. Which powerful blond striker scored both West Germany's goals in their 1980 European Championship Final win over Belgium?
4. Who was Scotland's manager during the 1986 World Cup Finals in Mexico?
5. What were the colours of Leeds United before Don Revie became manager?
6. If a forward hits an indirect free-kick into the net, what should be given?

QUIZ 336

1. What was the significance of Pat Van den Hauwe's goal for Everton at Norwich in May 1987?
2. Name the member of Sunderland's 1973 FA Cup-winning side who appeared as a substitute for Manchester City in the 1981 Final.
3. Whose goal for Italy ended England's 1980 European Championship hopes in Turin?
4. Which South American country plays in red shirts, blue shorts and white socks?
5. Other than Hampden, which was the last ground to host a Scotland home match?
6. Melwood is the training ground of which top club?

QUIZ 337

1. Name the Hearts captain who was sent off in the 1986 Scottish Cup Final with Aberdeen.
2. Newcastle lost 3-0 to Liverpool in the 1974 FA Cup Final. Two of their players that day later joined the Anfield club - name either.
3. In 1983 at Wembley, which country beat England for the first time, ending their European Championship hopes?
4. Who was the English referee who officiated in the 1986 World Cup?
5. Which BBC racing commentator is a fan of Swindon Town?
6. Of which position was Walter Winterbottom the first incumbent?

QUIZ 338

1. Why did Ossie Ardiles miss out on Spurs' 1982 FA Cup triumph?
2. Which transfer barrier did Alf Common break in 1905?
3. Name the Dutchman who was three times voted European Footballer of the Year.
4. Which South American country had two players sent off in their 1966 World Cup quarter-final match?
5. Barry McGuigan won his first World Title fight at which London soccer ground?
6. What have Bert Turner and Tommy Hutchison both done in FA Cup Finals?

QUIZ 339

1. Which Edinburgh team once had a forward-line known as the 'Famous Five'?
2. When Manchester United's Kevin Moran was sent off in the 1985 FA Cup Final, which striker took his position as an emergency defender?
3. Which country eliminated England from the 1968 European Championship thanks to a Dragan Dzajic goal?
4. Where was the 1986 Cup originally intended to be held?
5. The title of Phil Neal's autobiography is a parody of 'Life at the Top' - what slight change did he make to that title?
6. Where else, apart from Merseyside, could you watch a team called Everton?

---------------------- **QUIZ 340** ----------------------

1. Which club, now in the Scottish Second Division, won six of the first nine Scottish Cups?
2. Who was the Dublin-born university graduate who starred for Liverpool in the 1970s?
3. For which country did 35-year-old Wilfred Van Moer star in the 1980 European Championship Finals?
4. In what way are the international careers of Brian Stein, Danny Wallace and Nigel Spink similar?
5. Why did Jack Charlton turn down the captaincy at Leeds United?
6. In which Brazilian city does the Corinthians club play?

---------------------- **QUIZ 341** ----------------------

1. Who led Berwick to victory over Rangers in the 1966-67 Scottish Cup and later became manager at Ibrox?
2. Who was the Fulham star of the 1960s who demonstrated the merits of 'Brylcream' hair gel?
3. Which Hamburg star was European Footballer of the Year in 1978 and 1979?
4. What is the name of the suburb of Mexico City where Scotland played two of their matches in the 1986 World Cup?
5. In 1985, what was the hair-raising device which Chelsea wanted to use to stop pitch invasions?
6. Which wage barrier did Fulham's Johnny Haynes break?

---------------------- **QUIZ 342** ----------------------

1. Name the manager who took Manchester City to the 1981 FA Cup Final.
2. Who, in 1959, became the first Englishman to win 100 caps?
3. Which unfancied national side reached the 1980 European Championship Finals and held eventual winners West Germany to a no-score draw?
4. Name either of the countries for which centre-half Louis Monti played in World Cup Finals during the 1930s.
5. Which Victorian hymn is traditionally sung before Wembley FA Cup Finals?
6. Can any player take a goal kick?

QUIZ 343

1. In 1938, which Fife team became the only Second Division winners of the Scottish Cup to date?
2. Who kept goal for Everton in the 1986 FA Cup Final with Liverpool?
3. Who scored Liverpool's goal in the 1984 European Cup Final against Roma?
4. Who were the 'rabbits' who held Scotland to a 1-1 draw in the 1978 World Cup?
5. Which Midlands team does comedian Lenny Henry follow?
6. Which country failed to get one shot at England's goal during the entire ninety minutes of a 1971 match at Wembley?

QUIZ 344

1. For which team did Dixie Deans score a Scottish Cup Final hat-trick in 1972?
2. Which Bolton Wanderers forward was the top First Division scorer in 1978-79?
3. Which nation won the 1968 European Championship, beating Yugoslavia in the Rome Final?
4. What are the colours of Sweden's strip?
5. Which famous trophy was made of solid gold, weighed approximately nine pounds and stood only one foot high?
6. In Wembley Charity Shield matches, have the League Champions or the FA Cup holders won more often?

QUIZ 345

1. Which team won three consecutive Scottish Cups from 1982 to 1984?
2. Who is the only man to play and score for both Everton and Liverpool in Merseyside derbies?
3. Which country did Spain refuse to play in the 1960 Nations Cup because of its involvement in the Spanish Civil War?
4. Who won the Golden Ball award for being voted top player of the 1978 World Cup Tournament?
5. If you travelled down Cold Blow Lane to 'The Den', which team would you be going to see?
6. What unimpressive record does the Stockport-Leicester City match of May 1921 hold?

QUIZ 346

1. In the early years of the Football League, which Northern club were nicknamed 'The Invincibles'?
2. Who was the ex-Manchester City goalkeeper who died in the Munich air crash while covering the match for his newspaper?
3. In which European country does the team 17 Nentori play?
4. Did veteran captain Bobby Moore ever score a goal for England?
5. What was the crowd phenomenon which became a common feature at matches during the 1986 World Cup?
6. Can a goal be scored directly from a corner-kick?

QUIZ 347

1. Jeff Astle's goal won the 1968 FA Cup for which team?
2. Who was the powerful Liverpool centre-half of the 1960s who sampled managment at Tranmere?
3. Which club provided six players for West Germany's 1972 European Championship side?
4. When was the last time that all four British national sides qualified for the World Cup Finals?
5. In which stadium did the New York Cosmos play?
6. Can an injured player, after receiving treatment on the touchline return to the field while the game is still in progress?

QUIZ 348

1. In 1979, goalkeeper Ray Clemence and his Liverpool team-mates established the record for the fewest goals ever conceded in a First Division season. Was it 16, 20 or 24?
2. Who was the first black player to play for England?
3. Against which country did Gerd Muller score twice to enable West Germany to win the 1972 European Championship in Brussels?
4. Which country won the Veterans World Cup Tournament, for players over 34 years old, held in Brazil during January and February of 1989?
5. Cambridge United play in which colours?
6. Despite being top Division One goalscorer, why was 1973-74 not a particularly happy season for Mick Channon?

QUIZ 349

1. Who scored Celtic's 1980 Scottish Cup Final winner, later playing for Leeds and Hibernian?
2. Who kept goal for Arsenal's 'Double'-winning side of 1970-71?
3. Which home nation reached the quarter-finals of the 1976 European Championship losing in a two-leg tie with Yugoslavia?
4. From which country did top international referee Abraham Klein come?
5. For which football club did Yorkshire and England wicket-keeper David Bairstow play five League matches in 1971-72?
6. Who were the Club Champions of the World for 1988?

QUIZ 350

1. Ian 'Saint' St John once bossed which South Coast club?
2. Name Manchester United's international goalkeeper who was forced out of top-class football by a knee injury in 1987.
3. Which Cologne striker came on as a substitute for West Germany in the 1976 European Championship semi-final and proceeded to score a hat-trick?
4. Where are the headquarters of FIFA?
5. At which ground might you smell the Colmans Mustard works?
6. Name the goalkeeper who, in 1988, joined Leicester from Sheffield Wednesday where he had previously set a new club record for consecutive appearances.

QUIZ 351

1. Name the full-back who captained Celtic to Scottish Cup victories in 1980 and 1985.
2. In May 1989, who became the first-ever Wimbledon player to be capped for England?
3. Who was the centre-half who scored Liverpool's vital third goal in their first-leg UEFA Cup Final win over Moenchengladbach in 1973?
4. Has a South American country ever won the World Cup in Europe?
5. Which Staffordshire ground was planned in 1950 to be the 'Wembley of the North'?
6. Which English club has won the Welsh Cup on six occasions?

QUIZ 352

1. Name the striker, now playing in France, who scored for Aberdeen in the 1983 and 1984 Scottish Cup Finals.
2. In the 1970s, who was the Arsenal striker who became a Liverpool midfielder?
3. Which 'minnow' country did Spain beat 12-1 to eliminate Holland on goal-difference from the 1984 European Championships - Cyprus, Luxembourg or Malta?
4. What do the Italians call the sweeper in their teams?
5. Whose autobiography is entitled *When The Going Gets Tough*?
6. Which First Division goalkeeper scored against Sheffield Wednesday in October 1986?

QUIZ 353

1. How did Rangers win two Skol Cup Finals in 1984?
2. During the 1970s, Bruce Rioch and Colin Todd, later to become Middlesbrough's management team, played together at which First Division club?
3. Which country did France beat to win the 1984 European Championship in Paris?
4. Name the four countries with which Manchester United had players in the 1986 World Cup.
5. Which Liverpool player's pre-match routine involves kicking the ball against the light-switch until the light goes out?
6. From which Scottish club did Chelsea sign Stevie Clarke in 1987?

QUIZ 354

1. At which ground did Dundee United win the 1979 and 1980 Scottish League Cups?
2. Who was the Southern League player who won BBC's 1971-72 'Goal of the Season' for his legendary FA Cup strike against Newcastle?
3. Top Greek side OFI play on which popular holiday island?
4. For which of the home nations was Aston Villa winger Peter McParland the leading scorer in the 1958 World Cup?
5. Which other sport did Fulham stage at their Craven Cottage ground during the 1980s?
6. What was the score in the drawn Leicester-Arsenal match of 1930?

QUIZ 355

1. Name the England international who scored for QPR in the 1982 FA Cup Final against his present club Tottenham.
2. Who is the former England winger who has played for Manchester City, West Bromwich, Leeds, Real Betis, Coventry and Manchester United?
3. Name the blond, long-haired German midfielder who tore England apart in a 1972 European Championship match at Wembley.
4. Which team finished third in the 1966 World Cup won by England?
5. What colour is the Derby County jersey?
6. Why was Luton's Ashley Grimes sent off against Norwich in March 1987?

QUIZ 356

1. Which other Glasgow team caused a sensation by defeating Celtic 4-1 in the 1971 Scottish League Cup Final?
2. Who is the Rod Stewart look-alike striker who played League football for Cambridge, Derby, Everton, Portsmouth and Brighton?
3. What was the name of the ultra-defensive system which originated in Italy during the 1960s?
4. Which country had stars Toroscik and Nyilasi sent off against Argentina in the 1978 World Cup?
5. Top non-League club Altrincham is situated on the outskirts of which major city?
6. Who was Bradford City manager from 1987 to 1989?

QUIZ 357

1. Name the powerhouse defender, recently with Shrewsbury and Fulham, who was ordered off in the 1978-79 Scottish League Cup Final while playing for Aberdeen.
2. Who is the full-back, originally joining Luton on the YTS, who followed manager David Pleat to Spurs in 1986?
3. What are the colours of Locomotiv Leipzig?
4. After the Charltons in 1966, who were the next pair of brothers to play together in a World Cup Final?
5. For which soccer club did Worcestershire cricketer Ted Hemsley play?
6. In which country is the River Plate stadium?

QUIZ 358

1. Who is the current Dundee manager who scored the winner for the club in the 1973-74 Scottish League Cup Final against Celtic?
2. For which First Division side did Brendon Batson play from 1978 to 1982?
3. Which two Englishman opposed each other in the 1980 Cologne-Hamburg Bundesliga match?
4. How many Arsenal players turned out for England against Italy in 1934?
5. Which former England Under-21 star made a public appeal to play for Scotland in 1987?
6. Which team always plays in the European Cup?

QUIZ 359

1. What was the rather unfair nickname of Arsenal's successful team of the 1930s?
2. Danny McGrain and Gary Mabbutt have both successfully overcome which handicap in pursuing their football careers?
3. Ralf Edstroem who played in Holland for PSV was an international cap for which country?
4. Who managed Brazil's 1970 World Cup-winning team?
5. Who was the Arsenal full-back who once dropped his shorts in a gesture to fans?
6. Which Arsenal star was voted PFA Young Player of the Year in 1987?

QUIZ 360

1. With which team did Joe Harper win a Scottish Cup medal in the 3-1 defeat of Celtic in 1970?
2. Who was the 16-year-old who scored twelve goals in eight matches for Birmingham in 1971?
3. With which club was Santillana a prolific scorer in the 1970s and 80s?
4. Who was the only Glasgow Rangers player to appear in the 1982 World Cup?
5. Who received the Milk Cup Trophy after Liverpool had beaten Manchester United in 1983?
6. Name the young Liverpool defender who scored in his first Anfield League appearance against Nottingham Forest in April 1987.

QUIZ 361
---

1. Which Aberdeen striker netted twice in their 1986 Scottish Cup Final defeat of Hearts?
2. With which team did defender Tommy Booth win League and Cup medals?
3. West German manager Franz Beckenbauer captained which club side to European Cup success in the 1970s?
4. In which colour of shirts did England win the World Cup in 1966?
5. About whom did Don Revie say 'When he plays on snow - he doesn't leave any footprints'?
6. Why did Liverpool's 3-2 victory over Arsenal in 1964 get the attention of the nation?

QUIZ 362
---

1. When did Wolves last play in Division One - 1980, 1982 or 1984?
2. With which club did international striker Tony Woodcock shoot to fame?
3. Italian World Cup striker Giorgio Chinaglia became a scoring sensation with which American team?
4. Which country won gold in the 1988 Olympic Football Tournament in Seoul?
5. Which team plays at Kenilworth Road?
6. Tommy Docherty, Ian Porterfield and Emlyn Hughes have all been manager at which club?

QUIZ 363
---

1. Which Scottish city had both its clubs in the 1980-81 Scottish League Cup Final?
2. Name the Welsh international goalkeeper who became Sunderland's record signing when they paid £450,000 to Hull in December 1988.
3. For which country did Florian Albert star in the 1960s?
4. Which England veteran of 106 internationals won his final cap against West Germany in the Mexico World Cup of 1970?
5. Which outspoken First Division manager described England's 1980 strip as being 'like one of my mother's pinnies'?
6. How did Graeme Souness 'commemorate' his Scottish League debut at Easter Road in August 1986?

QUIZ 364

1. Name the World Cup star who was the first player to appear as a substitute in Scottish senior football.
2. Which First Division goalkeeper plays Minor Counties cricket for Shropshire?
3. Amaro Amancio played for and later managed which top European club?
4. What are the three colours of Hungary's strip?
5. Cardiff is one of the venues used for Welsh international matches - name the other two.
6. What was the result of Mark Reid's over-vigorous protest about a Norwich goal against his club Charlton in January 1987?

QUIZ 365

1. What record is held by John Hewitt's goal in the 1982 Scottish Cup match between Motherwell and Aberdeen?
2. Which team first brought Dutchman Romeo Zondervan to England in 1982?
3. Who, when joining Austrian club Vorwaerts Steyr in the spring of 1988, became the first 'big name' Soviet player to move abroad?
4. Which European country won the World Cup twice in the 1930s under the management of Vittorio Pozzo?
5. What was England's 1982 World Cup mascot called?
6. Which Liverpool defender broke his leg in the 1987 Littlewoods Cup quarter-final with Everton?

QUIZ 366

1. When were Arsenal last in Division Two - 1919, 1939 or 1959?
2. Who was the Newcastle and Sunderland inside-forward of the 1940s and 50s nicknamed the 'Clown Prince of Soccer'?
3. Jozef Bozsik was a Member of Parliament and a right-half for which country in the 1950s?
4. Who was the West Bromwich striker who almost snatched a dramatic equalizer for England in their 1970 World Cup classic encounter with Brazil?
5. Which Yorkshire side plays at Millmoor?
6. Pat Jennings record of 1098 appearances in senior British football was broken in April 1987 by which other top goal-keeper?

QUIZ 367

1. Name the Southampton forward who was top First Division goalscorer in 1979-80.
2. Which QPR striker hit 28 Division Two goals in 1979-80?
3. Who was Michel Platini's predecessor as the 'Golden Boy' of French football?
4. Glenn Hoddle scored on his international debut in 1979 - against which Eastern-bloc country were England playing?
5. Which Scottish side are known as 'The Jam Tarts'?
6. In 1980, which team beat Bristol City to become the only Scottish winners of the Anglo-Scottish Cup?

QUIZ 368

1. At which club did Mike Summerbee and Francis Lee star together in the 60s and 70s?
2. In 1979, which former England World Cup goalkeeper bought a hotel on the Scottish island of Mull and played part-time for Dundee United?
3. Where did Nottingham Forest beat Hamburg to lift their second European Cup in 1980?
4. Who scored West Germany's equalizer which looked as if it would take the 1986 World Cup Final into extra-time?
5. Which London club's motto is *Audere Est Facere*?
6. Do the UEFA Cup winners always defend the trophy?

QUIZ 369

1. Who is the only player to have captained both Scottish and FA Cup-winning teams?
2. Name the former schoolboy rugby international who joined Leicester City from Notts County in March 1989.
3. Which team bought Johan Cruyff from Ajax for £922,300 in 1973?
4. Europeans call him a technical director - what would we call him?
5. Which ITV panellist was in tears after watching Scotland being knocked out of the 1974 World Cup?
6. Graeme Souness' first major shock as a manager occurred when Rangers were knocked out of the 1987 Scottish Cup by which unfancied side?

---------------- **QUIZ 370** ----------------

1. Who captained Leeds United's Championship sides of 1969 and 1974?
2. In 1957, which Welshman became the first major British soccer export to Italy?
3. Florea Dumitrache was an international star for which Eastern European country?
4. Which defender won his 50th cap for England in the 1987 European Championship match against Northern Ireland in Belfast?
5. Which team did Edinburgh's Ferranti Thistle become on its admission to the Scottish League in 1974?
6. Which former League referee became Minister of Sport during the 1970s?

---------------- **QUIZ 371** ----------------

1. With which club did Alan Ball win his only League Championship medal as a player?
2. Birmingham defender of the 1970s Malcolm Page was an international for which country?
3. For which top Portuguese club did Eusebio play?
4. Against which less-distinguished footballing country did England play three games in June 1983?
5. Yorkshire vet Alf Wight shot to fame as a writer after taking his pen-name from which former Birmingham and Hibs goalkeeper?
6. In 1985-86, who competed in the Screen Sport Super Cup?

---------------- **QUIZ 372** ----------------

1. Who was captain of Manchester City's successful team of the late 1960s?
2. Name the England striker whose former clubs include Carlisle United, Vancouver Whitecaps and Newcastle United.
3. Brazilian World Cup star Falcao once played against Liverpool in a European Cup Final - for which club?
4. Which country scored its first-ever goal against England in a February 1989 friendly?
5. Who was the Celtic and Scotland winger known as 'Wee Jinky'?
6. At which club did Frank Casper replace Brian Miller as manager in 1989?

QUIZ 373

1. Which Midlands club did Mike Bailey captain to League Cup victory in 1974?
2. The famous England winger Tom Finney scored 187 League goals for which club?
3. Which manager guided teams to European Cup-Winners Cup success in 1987 and 1989?
4. Who was the England star who scored for the Rest of the World in the UNICEF match of 1986?
5. Which Second Division ground was used a prisoner-of-war camp during World War Two?
6. Why did Spurs pay AC Milan exactly £99,999 for Jimmy Greaves in 1962?

QUIZ 374

1. After many fruitful seasons at Maine Road, which club did striker Francis Lee help win the Championship in 1975?
2. Who was the last Manchester United player to be Footballer of the Year?
3. Which Soviet club thrashed Arsenal 5-2 at Highbury in the 1982-83 UEFA Cup?
4. Which London club provided both Scotland and Northern Ireland goalkeepers for the 1965 international in Belfast?
5. Which is the oldest League ground in England?
6. For what unusual reason did Liverpool's Jan Molby miss part of the 1988-89 season?

QUIZ 375

1. Who was captain of Celtic's all-conquering European Cup side of 1967?
2. Derek Fazackerley played for 16 years with which club before joining Chester in 1987?
3. For which country did Gorgon and Zmuda star in the 1970s?
4. Scotland beat England by 2-1 in both 1976 and 1977 - which Celtic forward scored the winner in both games?
5. What was the christian name of former Belgian international 'keeper Piot?
6. In the 1978 League Cup Final replay, which player was booked for the first time in his 800-match career?

QUIZ 376

1. George Eastham won a League Cup medal in 1972 - with which club?
2. With which London club did Scottish international Charlie Cooke make his name?
3. In 1974, Joachim Streich starred in which European nation's first World Cup Finals appearance?
4. For which country was Sandor Kocsis, known as 'Golden Head', the leading scorer in the 1954 World Cup?
5. What was the collective nickname of 1970s Bristol Rovers strikers Bruce Bannister and Alan Warboys?
6. Who selects the Footballer of the Year?

QUIZ 377

1. Len Glover played for which club when they lost the 1969 FA Cup Final?
2. Goalkeeper Joe Corrigan had a highly successful career with which club?
3. Which colour is common to the strip of Anderlecht and FK Austria Vienna?
4. Who took over from Alf Ramsey as England manager?
5. In 1979, which soccer star reached the top of the German pop charts with 'Head Over Heels in Love'?
6. In August 1987, Southampton signed a West Bromwich full-back, whose proposed transfer to Liverpool in the previous season had fallen through on medical grounds - can you name him?

QUIZ 378

1. Which team did long-serving centre-half Colin Jackson help win two Scottish 'Trebles' during the 1970s?
2. Which defender, who joined Leeds from Watford in 1989, has played league football in all four home countries?
3. Arie Haan, who managed Stuttgart to the 1989 UEFA Cup Final, starred in the 1974 and 1978 World Cups for which country?
4. Which famous international footballer scored his 1000th goal in the Santos-Vasco de Gama match of 1969?
5. What was the name of the Adidas ball used for the 1986 World Cup?
6. Before joining Coventry, John Sillett was manager at which club?

QUIZ 379

1. Who headed the winning goal for Rangers in the 1970 Scottish League Cup Final at the age of only 16?
2. In which country was England Under-21 full-back Tony Dorigo born?
3. Arnold Muhren's brother Gerrie won three European Cup medals with which club?
4. Which West German star played out the 1970 World Cup semi-final with his arm in a sling?
5. At which ground would you find the Gallowgate End and the Leazes Park End?
6. Which French club did Mo Johnston join in 1987?

QUIZ 380

1. With which club did Joe Jordan win a League Championship medal in 1974?
2. Name the young Manchester United star who, at 17, became the youngest player ever to appear for the England Under-21 side when he made his debut against Greece in February 1989.
3. Who was the Derby County striker ordered off against Juventus in the 1973 European Cup?
4. Where will the 1994 World Cup be held?
5. What is the title of FIFA's official film of the 1986 World Cup?
6. Who is the former Scotland striker who led Bristol City to the 1989 Littlewoods Cup semi-finals?

QUIZ 381

1. Which goalkeeper scored with a long kick-out in the 1967 Manchester United-Spurs Charity Shield match?
2. As well as midfield, in which position has Bryan Robson played for England?
3. For which team did Francisco Gento appear in more than 80 European Cup ties, gaining six winners medals?
4. Former Chelsea boss John Hollins was an England international, but for which country was his brother David capped?
5. Who is the West Indian cricket star who played in the 1978 World Cup qualifying tournament for Antigua?
6. Which leading First Division boss began his management career at East Stirlingshire?

QUIZ 382

1. Ross Jenkins was Division Three's top goalscorer in 1978-79 - which club was he playing for?
2. Between 1979 and 1981, Nottingham Forest three times spent £1 million on a striker - can you name the players concerned?
3. Which team did Nandor Hidegkuti help defeat England at Wembley in 1953?
4. In which year did Peter Shilton first play for England - 1970, 1972 or 1974?
5. Which Football League club has a Findus Stand?
6. On the England Under-21 shirt, which word was traditionally embroidered beneath the crest?

QUIZ 383

1. David Jack, in 1928, became the first player to be transferred for which then record sum?
2. Name the former Luton midfielder who made his only appearance for England in Paris in 1984.
3. What change did Spurs traditionally make to their strip when playing in a European match?
4. With 13 goals, Just Fontaine was the leading scorer in the 1958 World Cup - for which country did he play?
5. Kilmarnock FC was originally founded to play which sport?
6. Which team won the inaugural four-club Wembley International tournament in August 1988?

QUIZ 384

1. Whom did George Graham replace as Arsenal boss in 1986?
2. Name the Brighton forward who played on loan for his old club Rangers in the 1982 Scottish League Cup Final at Hampden.
3. Who was the top European goal-snatcher nicknamed 'Der Bomber'?
4. Who, in 1960, became the first Scottish League player to appear for England?
5. What are the colours of Mansfield Town?
6. What is the referee's signal for an indirect free-kick?

QUIZ 385

1. Which Southampton striker was the First Division's leading goalscorer in 1981-82?
2. Diminutive midfielder Ray Train had many clubs - but for which of them did he play in the 1974-75 First Division?
3. Who was the athletic Dutch midfielder of the 1970s who played for Ajax, Barcelona and New York Cosmos?
4. Which nation won the 1954 World Cup despite losing 8-3 in a first round match?
5. What is Glasgow Rangers' worst-ever league position?
6. What was remarkable about Kevin Dillon's hat-trick for Portsmouth in 1986?

QUIZ 386

1. How many goals did Kevin Keegan score against Everton in Merseyside derby matches?
2. Which top Spanish club signed Bangor striker Vivian Williams after he impressed against them in 1985?
3. Name the top player who began his career with Nancy, where he used to practise bending free-kicks round a line of wooden dummies.
4. When Kenny Dalglish became Scotland's most capped player, whose record did he beat?
5. 'The Shed' is a famous part of which ground?
6. After a goal has been awarded, can a referee change his decision?

QUIZ 387

1. Who was the Everton and England marksman who was the First Division's top scorer in 1977-78?
2. In the summer of 1988, which team did Northern Ireland striker Jimmy Quinn join, thus ending his second spell with Swindon Town?
3. Bruno Pezzey is a much-capped international star for which country?
4. Which was the first country to defeat England during their reign as World Champions?
5. Which team were known as the 'Biscuitmen' because of their close proximity to a Huntly and Palmer's factory?
6. Why were Luton ejected from the Littlewoods Cup in 1986?

QUIZ 388

1. Manchester United's relegation in 1974 was sealed when which of their former stars back-heeled the winner for Manchester City in the Old Trafford derby?
2. From which club did Rangers sign winger Mark Walters?
3. Who was the Austrian striker signed by Barcelona after impressive displays in the 1978 World Cup?
4. Whom did Jack Charlton succeed as Eire boss?
5. At which Yorkshire ground was the pitch moved 30 feet during major redevelopments in the 1970s?
6. What was the score in the League Cup ties between West Ham and Bury in 1983 and Liverpool and Fulham in 1986?

QUIZ 389

1. With which club did West Ham boss Lou Macari play in three FA Cup Finals?
2. Who was the England centre-half of the 1970s who played for Sunderland, Manchester City, Werder Bremen and Southampton?
3. Which Football League club signed Swiss star Raimondo Ponte from Grasshoppers in 1980?
4. Which of these England managers won the most caps as a player - Alf Ramsey, Don Revie or Bobby Robson?
5. Actor Tom Watt, who played 'Lofty' in 'Eastenders', is nuts about which team?
6. Merseyside-based Leasowe Pacific won which national competition in 1989?

QUIZ 390

1. Who struck the penalty which won the 1982 FA Cup for Spurs?
2. Which Arsenal, Manchester United and Scotland defender of the 1960s had a three-letter surname?
3. For which team did winger Carlos Rexach play in the Cup-Winners Cup Finals of 1969 and 1979?
4. Who was the Blackburn Rovers winger who appeared in the 1982 World Cup for Northern Ireland?
5. In 1987, which Liverpool player wrote a musical tribute to his club entitled 'Pride of Merseyside'?
6. Name the former Spurs full-back who was appointed Torquay boss in 1987 after four years in charge at Darlington.

QUIZ 391

1. Who managed Derby County to the Championship in 1975, having previously won a League medal as a Spurs player in 1961?
2. Ray Crawford was top First Division scorer in 1962 - with which club was he playing?
3. Roland Sandberg was a World Cup star for which European country?
4. Which country beat red-hot favourites Brazil to lift the 1950 World Cup in Rio?
5. What are the colours of St Mirren?
6. Why did the chairman of Bournemouth and Boscombe Athletic change the club's name to AFC Bournemouth in 1971?

QUIZ 392

1. Who was Nottingham Forest's captain in their Championship team of 1978?
2. West Ham signed defender Julian Dicks from which club in 1988?
3. Andre Szarmach starred in the 1974 World Cup - for which country?
4. Name any two of the three Spurs players who appeared in the 1982 World Cup and the countries for which they played.
5. Where did England acclimatise for the 1986 World Cup?
6. Which of Coventry's goalscorers in the 1987 FA Cup Final had previously lost to Spurs in the 1981 Final?

QUIZ 393

1. Who skippered Aston Villa to League Championship success in 1980-81?
2. Who was the highly-skilled forward, nicknamed 'Roy of the Rovers' who played for Forest, Leeds, Anderlecht, Everton, Chelsea and Blackburn?
3. Dutch international midfielder Wim Van Hanegem helped which club beat Spurs in the 1974 UEFA Cup Final?
4. Name one of the three Arsenal players who made their England debuts in the 1-1 draw against Saudi Arabia in November 1988.
5. What are the colours of Forfar Athletic?
6. In 1978, who became the first man to appear in a Wembley Cup Final without having played in a League match for his club?

QUIZ 394

1. Name the captain of Derby County's 1972 Championship side.
2. Defender George Berry, a five-times Welsh cap, was born in which country?
3. Who was the Dutch World Cup striker who played for the French club Bastia when they lost the 1978 UEFA Cup Final to PSV Eindhoven?
4. Who was England's 'B' Team manager when Ron Greenwood was in charge of the national side?
5. What unusual landmark is situated in one corner of Goodison Park?
6. The 1969 Footballer of the Year award was shared by the captains of Manchester City and Derby County. Name either player.

QUIZ 395

1. Name the Manchester City full-back, later to become a coach at the club, who scored the winning goal in the 1970 League Cup Final.
2. Who was the Chester striker who scored four goals on his full debut for Wales in October 1978?
3. What is the surname of the brothers Rene and Willy who played together for PSV Eindhoven and Holland?
4. Name the Spurs and Fulham midfielder, later a successful manager at Brighton, who was the first England player to be sent off in a full international.
5. What unusual colour did Liverpool adopt for their change strip in 1987?
6. Since 1986, in which town would you have watched Bristol Rovers play their home matches?

QUIZ 396

1. Former Leeds and England boss Don Revie played in the 1955 and 1956 FA Cup Finals - for which team?
2. Who played in both the English and Scottish League Cup Finals during 1985 - for Sunderland and Hibernian respectively?
3. In 1988-89, which other Bundesliga team shared the Neckarstadion with VfB Stuttgart?
4. Hector Chumpitaz played in 150 games and two World Cups for which South American country?
5. Which of the Manchester grounds has the largest pitch in British football?
6. In 1987, who was the First Division's top goalscorer and both the PFA and Football Writers' Player of the Year?

QUIZ 397

1. John Richards' goal won a League Cup Final during the 1970s - for which team?
2. Which Reading striker scored four goals against Doncaster in September 1982 yet still finished on the losing side in a 7-5 defeat?
3. Which Italian goalkeeper won 112 caps between 1968 and 1983?
4. In the 1982 World Cup, which team walked off the pitch in disgust after France had been awarded a controversial goal?
5. At which ground might you sit in the Bob Lord Stand?
6. Which former manager took over as caretaker Sunderland boss on the departure of Lawrie McMenemy in 1987?

QUIZ 398

1. Who captained Liverpool to three consecutive League Titles from 1982?
2. John Gregory, who took over as Portsmouth manager in 1989, is an international cap for which country?
3. Gianni Rivera, Italian midfield star of four World Cups, played for which major club?
4. Which England goalkeeper allowed a Kenny Dalglish shot through his legs to give Scotland victory in the 1976 Home International match?
5. Which colour of ball was used in the 1966 World Cup Final?
6. How much was the referee's fee for a Football League match in 1988-89 - £60, £80 or £100?

QUIZ 399

1. Who captained Liverpool's 1973 League Championship side?
2. Who was the striker, signed by West Bromwich for £480,000 in 1979, who scored only six League goals for the club in four years?
3. For which player did Inter-Milan pay Bayern Munich over £2 million in 1984?
4. Which African nation thrashed Italy 4-0 in the Seoul Olympics?
5. Which top British film personality was once a director of Chelsea?
6. Why are 'derby matches' so called?

QUIZ 400

1. Which famous Liverpool manager played in Preston's successful 1938 FA Cup Final team?
2. In 1981 Tony Morley won a League Championship medal with which club?
3. Which European country had over a hundred Brazilian players in its 1988-89 First Division?
4. Jesper Olsen, who played for Manchester United from 1984 to 1988, is a full international for which country?
5. How did bookmakers William Hill show their feelings about Maradona's controversial first goal in the 1986 World Cup match against England?
6. Wine-bar owner and part-time goalkeeper Gary Plumley played one game for Watford in 1987 - can you remember which one?

QUIZ 401

1. Bobby Tambling scored the only goal for which team in their 1967 FA Cup Final defeat by Spurs?
2. Who was the 21-year-old Manchester United wing-half who had already won 18 England caps when he was tragically killed at Munich in 1958?
3. In which position did the famous Russian Lev Yashin play?
4. In the 1986 World Cup, which country had players sent off in their group matches with Denmark and Scotland?
5. How many League clubs does London have - eight, ten or twelve?
6. Which Football League club has, on average, attracted most fans in the past fifteen years?

QUIZ 402

1. Which team defeated Arsenal in a thrilling Final to lift the 1988 Littlewoods Cup?
2. Who was the Chelsea No.9 who hit five goals against Juenesse Hautcharage in the 1971-72 Cup-Winners Cup?
3. Paul Van Himst played international soccer for which European country?
4. Which Dutchman was top scorer in the 1988 European Championship Finals?
5. Whose autobiography is entitled *Both Sides of the Border*?
6. Which club's former managers include Tommy Docherty, Dave Sexton and Gordon Jago?

QUIZ 403

1. Which club axed Jim Smith as manager in February 1982?
2. Which Second Division club did Mark Hateley leave to go to Italy in 1984?
3. Anton Ondrus was a star defender for which Eastern European national side?
4. Who were the only past winners not to compete in the 1981 *Mundialito* mini-World Cup in Uruguay?
5. In the 'Brookside' TV series, which team does the character Terry Sullivan support?
6. What did Real Madrid not do at home for eight years from 1957 to 1965?

QUIZ 404

1. Which team, now in Division Three, claimed five First Division scalps on their way to winning the 1988 Simod Cup?
2. Which famous goalkeeper's first honour was skippering the Leicester school's XI while playing at right-half?
3. Who is the Dane who has scored in the finals of all three major European tournaments?
4. What was the score of the first Scotland-England match?
5. Who was it not unusual to see in the Swindon line-up during 1988-89?
6. What is a 'banana' shot?

QUIZ 405

1. Dennis Viollet was the top First Division goalscorer in 1960 - for which club did he play?
2. Full-back Alec Lindsay starred for which club during the 1970s?
3. Who was the Real Madrid star nicknamed the 'Galloping Major'?
4. Who is the former Arsenal and Aston Villa goalkeeper whose England career lasted only 45 minutes?
5. 'If he was a chocolate drop, he'd eat himself' - said Archie Gemmill of whom?
6. What is the usual method of restarting a game after a temporary suspension of play?

QUIZ 406

1. Which Manchester United star scored six goals in the 8-2 FA Cup defeat of Northampton in February 1970?
2. For which club did winger George Armstrong make 500 League appearances between 1960 and 1977?
3. Why is Eintracht Frankfurt against Vorwaerts Frankfurt not a local derby match?
4. Which of these players has never been capped for England - Mark Barham, John Gregory or Paul Power?
5. At which ground is the Kemlyn Road Stand?
6. Which was the last club to win the FA Cup with a team comprised entirely of Englishmen?

QUIZ 407

1. Liverpool's first League defeat of 1987-88 came in March of that season - which team beat them 1-0?
2. For which London side did Barry Kitchener play over 500 League games from 1967 to 1982?
3. After the 1971 European Cup success, Ajax manager Rinus Michels left to take charge of which Spanish club?
4. Which European country beat eventual winners Argentina 1-0 in a group match of the 1978 World Cup?
5. Name the Scottish Premier side which plays at Love Street, Paisley.
6. Which former Wales manager masterminded Egypt's success in the 1986 African Nations Cup?

QUIZ 408

1. Who was the first player to score 100 goals for a single club in both Scotland and England?
2. Name the midfielder who joined Fulham on a free-transfer from West Ham in June 1982.
3. From which Belgian club did Spurs sign Nico Claesen in 1986?
4. Name the English-born, Leeds United goalkeeper who played for Scotland in the 1974 World Cup.
5. What *faux-pas* did Spurs make with their playing kit in the 1987 FA Cup Final?
6. Name the former England skipper appointed player-manager of Bristol Rovers in July 1987.

QUIZ 409

1. Which player won Scottish Cup medals with both Celtic and Rangers during the 1970s?
2. Who was Wolves' Irish international striker of the 1970s who later became chairman of the club?
3. For which club has powerful Belgian international striker Jan Ceulemans starred since 1978?
4. Which was the first non-British national team to win in England?
5. Who is the TV entertainer who used to play for Northampton Town colts team?
6. By what name was the Sherpa Van Trophy previously known?

QUIZ 410

1. Which goalkeeper played in five FA Cup Finals from 1971 to 1987?
2. Which former England manager won a League Championship medal with Chelsea in 1955?
3. Which team defeated Bayern Munich to lift the 1987 European Cup?
4. Who was the Cameroons striker whose elation turned to dispair when his 1982 World Cup goal against Italy was ruled off-side?
5. What was the title of Arsenal FC's 1971 hit record based on the 'Rule Britannia' tune?
6. Which English referee took charge of the opening match of the 1988 European Championships?

QUIZ 411

1. Which club finished bottom of the 1988-89 First Division?
2. Who was the Barnet player sent off in an FA Cup first round match with Woking in 1978?
3. Which tournament do the Dutch call the *Europacup II*?
4. Name the brothers who played in Holland's victorious 1988 European Championship team.
5. In which Potteries town does Port Vale play?
6. Who had the longest career of any Football League player?

QUIZ 412

1. Nick Holmes scored for which team in the League Cup Final of 1979?
2. Who was the Luton Town first-choice goalkeeper who missed the 1988 Littlewoods Cup Final through injury?
3. For which top European side did Emilio Butragueno star in 1988-89?
4. Who was the powerfully-built, long-haired, moustachioed centre-forward of Argentina's 1978 World Cup team?
5. Into which singing family did former Torquay United captain Brian Wilson marry?
6. Which club regained its League status by winning the 1987-88 Vauxhall Conference?

QUIZ 413

1. Which team did John Greig captain in the 1970s?
2. Which successful Liverpool manager won an FA Amateur Cup medal with Bishop Auckland in 1939?
3. In the 1987 Cup Winners Cup Final, Ajax defeated a team from the German Democratic Republic (East Germany) - which team?
4. Which country has won the most Central American championships?
5. What are the famous colours of Motherwell FC?
6. Can a goal be scored directly from a kick-off?

QUIZ 414

1. Name one of the three First Division marksmen who scored a hat-trick on the opening day of the 1988-89 season.
2. Mohamed Ali Amar, Spurs' 1989 signing from Barcelona, is better known by what name?
3. In which European national team's line-up might you see Barros and Gomes?
4. Which European national side has the letters *DDR* on its jersey?
5. Michael Parkinson enjoys relating tales of spectating at which Yorkshire club?
6. What European feat has been achieved by Aberdeen, Manchester City, Rangers and West Ham?

QUIZ 415

1. Name either of the clubs which contested the 1989 Sherpa Van Trophy Final.
2. Name the striker from the Scottish Premier League who scored a World Cup goal against Wales in October 1988.
3. What is the surname of West German international brothers Klaus and Thomas?
4. Which Central American team did Hungary trounce 10-1 in the 1982 World Cup Tournament?
5. Irving Scholar is chairman of which leading English club?
6. Name either of the 1989 FA Trophy Finalists.

QUIZ 416

1. Which Hibernian player once scored a Scottish League Cup Final hat-trick but still finished on the losing side?
2. Which team did Kenny Burns join on leaving Forest in 1981?
3. Which club has won the European Cup most often?
4. In which German city was the 1988 European Championship Final between Holland and the Soviet Union played?
5. What is the name of the home of Derby County?
6. What is the maximum number of steps which a goalkeeper may take after receiving possession of the ball?

QUIZ 417

1. Which top First Division club did Irish boss Billy Bingham once manage?
2. Name the Newcastle-born striker who has played in the Midlands for Leicester, Notts County, Forest, Derby and Walsall.
3. Name the goalkeeper internationalist who joined Bayern Munich from Beveren in 1982.
4. Who scored Italy's goal in the 1970 World Cup Final?
5. Heart-throb singer Julio Iglesias was, at one time, youth team goalkeeper at which major club?
6. What is the 'Pools Panel'?

QUIZ 418

1. Which club did Bobby Robson manage before becoming England boss?
2. Name the former Celtic striker who was appointed assistant-manager of St Mirren in 1988.
3. Has a second division team ever won a European competition?
4. Which country has been World Cup runners-up most often?
5. Who led the fight for the abolition of the maximum wage for footballers?
6. Siggi Jonsson, who first played League football for Sheffield Wednesday in 1985, is an international for which country?

QUIZ 419

1. During 1988-89, which club did not win an away league match until they defeated Dundee United 1-0 on the last Saturday of the season?
2. Bobby Davison, who joined Leeds for £380,000 in November 1987, had been top scorer at which club in the previous five seasons?
3. Name the three Manchester United players who were each voted European Footballer of the Year during the 1960s.
4. Who was the England reserve goalkeeper heavily criticised after the 1970 World Cup defeat by West Germany?
5. Which well-known manager is a former guardsman?
6. What did Manchester City players Tony Adcock, Paul Stewart and David White all do in the match against Huddersfield in November 1987?

QUIZ 420

1. Whom did Howard Kendall succeed as Everton manager in 1981?
2. In the Scottish Cup semi-final of April 1988, who was the Dundee United centre-half sent off for the first time in his 16-year career, for a tackle on Charlie Nicholas?
3. The San Paolo stadium is home to which top Italian side?
4. Claudio Sulser helped defeat England in a 1981 World Cup qualifying match - with which country was he playing?
5. Who raised a few chuckles with his pronounciation of Gary Lineker's name during TV coverage of the 1986 World Cup?
6. What was the name of the Scottish pre-season knock-out tournament for high-scoring teams?

QUIZ 421

1. Who was the only Division One manager to be sacked during 1988-89?
2. Name the three clubs for which Asa Hartford appeared in League Cup Finals.
3. Who played in the Football League for Coventry and West Bromwich Albion before returning to his native Holland to captain Den Haag?
4. Name either of the Manchester City players in England's 1970 World Cup squad.
5. Who came on as substitute for Gary Stevens in the 1986 England-Scotland match at Wembley?
6. Which player has made the most all-time appearances for Manchester United?

QUIZ 422

1. At the end of the 1988-89 season, who was Scotland's longest-serving club manager?
2. Which North-Eastern club did Yugoslav Bosco Jankovic join in 1979?
3. Which team lifted the 1988 European Cup along with their own national championship and cup competition?
4. Which country competed with Scotland and England for the 1989 Rous Cup?
5. Which Nottingham Forest player is married to 'C.A.T.S. Eyes' actress Lesley Ash?
6. From where do the Wanderers of the GM Vauxhall Conference come?

QUIZ 423

1. Which club did Irishman John McClelland captain to Scottish Skol Cup success in 1984?
2. Which defender, twice an FA Cup medallist with Spurs, joined Watford from Charlton in a £85,000 deal during 1988?
3. Which West German international winger rejoined Cologne in 1987 after an unhappy 18-month spell with Racing Club of Paris?
4. In which colour of jersey does the Yugoslavian national team play?
5. Why was the singer Vince Hill a happy man on 16 May, 1987?
6. Which First Division club had the lowest average gate in 1988-89?

QUIZ 424

1. Whom did Kenny Dalglish succeed as manager of Liverpool?
2. Who is the Eire international full-back who left Birmingham to join his former boss Jim Smith at Oxford in 1984?
3. Name Hamburg's elegant West German international full-back who set a new Bundesliga appearance record when he played against Hannover in March 1989.
4. In 1930, what was Louis Laurent of France the first player ever to do?
5. Who said in 1982, 'Half a million for Remi Moses? You could get the original Moses plus the tablets for that price!'?
6. Who managed the Rest of the World side in the Football League centenary match of August 1987?

QUIZ 425

1. In 1989, which Rovers won the Scottish Second Division Championship thus gaining promotion for the first time in 40 years?
2. Who is 'Rocky' to the Arsenal fans?
3. In 1988 which Italian club paid £2.4 million to Bayern Munich for midfield dynamo Lothar Matthaus?
4. Apart from England, name two countries which have won the World Cup on their own soil.
5. Which item of players' equipment was first worn by Forest's Samuel Widdowson in 1874?
6. Which club sacked Bobby Ferguson as its manager in 1987?

QUIZ 426

1. First Division Coventry suffered a shock exit from the 1989 FA Cup at the hands of which non-League outfit?
2. Which striker joined Norwich from Rangers during the 1987-88 season?
3. Name the two leading European sides which Dundee United eliminated on their way to the 1987 UEFA Cup Final.
4. Who hit Argentina's winning goal in the 1986 World Cup Final?
5. What are the two colours of Wimbledon's strip?
6. Which national competition was won by Tamworth in 1989?

QUIZ 427

1. With which club did legendary Manchester United manager Matt Busby win an FA Cup medal as a player?
2. In Don Revie's famous Leeds team, who was the key utility man who played in almost every position?
3. Name the former Porto winger, known as 'Portugal's George Best', who captained Atletico Madrid during 1988-89.
4. Who is the only man to have played in and managed a World Cup-winning team?
5. What are the colours shared by Dunfermline, Grimsby and Notts County?
6. What is the lowest number of players ever used by a Football League Championship-winning team?

QUIZ 428

1. Which is the only club to have won all four divisions of the Football League?
2. Name the striker who returned to Hearts in December 1988 after an unsuccessful spell at Newcastle.
3. Which Belgian side won the 1988 European Cup-Winners Cup?
4. Which was the last country to win the World Cup with a 100% record?
5. Which team does actor Warren Mitchell follow?
6. What role does Fred Street perform for the England national team?

QUIZ 429

1. Which former Leeds and England defender was Bristol City manager from 1982 to 1988?
2. In July 1989, which Welshman moved 'Cities' from Coventry to Norwich?
3. For which club did Andoni Zubizarreta keep goal in a 1989 European tournament final?
4. What is the nickname of Australia's national team?
5. Which club's ground has a Babbacombe End?
6. Which former Liverpool hard-man was appointed boss of Caernarfon Town in 1987?

QUIZ 430

1. Which two English clubs have been managed by Celtic boss Billy McNeill?
2. Who was the star striker of the 1940s and 50s known as 'Morty'?
3. What is the significance of the red, white and green crest called a *scudetto* on the shirt of an Italian club?
4. Who was Scotland's 1982 World Cup skipper?
5. Which of the comedians Cannon and Ball was once chairman of Rochdale?
6. Who became Everton manager on the departure of Howard Kendall?

QUIZ 431

1. Who replaced Ron Atkinson as manager of Manchester United in 1986?
2. 1988-89 Notts County skipper Geoff Pike won an FA Cup winners medal with which club in 1980?
3. For which country is winger Wlodek Smolarek an international-ist?
4. Which key Soviet defender missed the 1988 European Championship Final after being yellow-carded in the semi-final?
5. Which other job did Mike England combine with managing Wales?
6. Which top Midlands club was managed during the 1970s by Sammy Chung?

QUIZ 432

1. Which Fourth Division side were League Cup runners-up in 1962?
2. Name the striker who played at Wembley for Brighton in 1983, Liverpool in 1984 and QPR in 1986, without ever finishing on a winning side.
3. PSV Eindhoven won the 1988 European Cup on a penalty shoot-out. Which team did they beat?
4. Who was the Liverpool midfield star who won his second cap against France in 1966 and his third cap eleven years later against Switzerland?
5. Whose idea was to build Liverpool into a 'Bastion of Invincibility'?
6. Can a goal be scored directly from a throw-in?

QUIZ 433

1. Name the manager who has been in charge at Aston Villa, Birmingham and West Bromwich Albion.
2. Name the former Sunderland goalkeeper who was signed by Sheffield Wednesday from Manchester United for a £175,000 fee in October 1988.
3. Who was the Belgian international striker signed by West Ham from New York Cosmos for £400,000 in 1982?
4. In which year was John Barnes first capped?
5. *Nil Satis Nisi Optimum* is the motto of which leading English club?
6. What variation on the off-side law was used in the Watney Cup competition?

QUIZ 434

1. Which Rangers striker scored a Skol Cup Final hat-trick against Celtic in 1984?
2. Name the striker who began his League career at Huddersfield in 1966 and since then played for ten other clubs, winning eight England caps along the way.
3. Who was the Athletic Bilbao defender who ended Maradona's season in 1983 with a scything tackle?
4. Which country finished third in the Mexico World Cup of 1986?
5. Cardinal Basil Hume supports which North-Eastern club?
6. Why is there an arc outside the penalty area?

QUIZ 435

1. Name the manager who guided Luton to two consecutive Littlewoods Cup Finals in the late 1980s.
2. Name the former Everton and Newcastle full-back who helped Bristol City reach the 1989 Littlewoods Cup semi-finals.
3. In what way is the Italian Cup Final different from the FA Cup Final?
4. Who became the 1000th English international when he came on as a substitute against West Germany in 1987?
5. Which of the Manchester clubs plays in the area called Moss Side?
6. What do managers Jock Wallace, Willie McFaul and Don Mackay have in common?

QUIZ 436

1. How many times has the FA Cup and League 'Double' been achieved?
2. Name the Scottish centre-half who lost to Aston Villa in the 1977 League Cup Final while with Everton, but went on to win League and European Cup medals with the Midlands club.
3. Whose near-post header won the 1987 Cup-Winners Cup for Ajax Amsterdam?
4. For which country did Antonio Carbajal keep goal in five World Cups from 1950 to 1966?
5. Which team plays at Molineux?
6. Which club has won the Scottish Cup more often - Clyde or Dundee United?

QUIZ 437

1. Which league did Dunfermline Athletic win in 1988-89?
2. Who is the Scottish midfielder who has played for Morton, Spurs, Bolton, Brighton and Manchester City?
3. Which German team knocked Celtic out of the 1988-89 European Cup on a 1-0 aggregate?
4. Which two neighbouring countries had never played each other in an international until 1978?
5. What feat have goalkeepers Peter Shilton, Pat Jennings and Steve Ogrizovic all performed?
6. Which Second Division club has been managed by Frank O'Farrell, Jimmy Bloomfield and Gordon Milne?

QUIZ 438

1. Other than Liverpool, which is the only team to have won the League Championship and League Cup in the same season?
2. Peter Mellor, Tommy Lawrence, John Hurst and Eric Martin - who is the odd man out?
3. Who captained Juventus' 1985 European Cup-winning side?
4. Name the two countries which were accused by Algeria of fixing the result of their 1982 World Cup match.
5. Which of the Bristol teams plays in blue and white quartered shirts?
6. Who was Brian Clough's predecessor at Nottingham Forest?

QUIZ 439

1. What was first played at Kennington Oval on 16 March 1872?
2. Don Megson captained Sheffield Wednesday in the 1966 FA Cup Final. What is the name of his son who played over 200 games for the club before joining Manchester City in January 1989?
3. In which country's leagues do most of Liechtenstein's clubs compete?
4. Who, in November 1987, became the first Hearts player in fourteen years to win an international cap?
5. As they run out for home matches, the Liverpool players touch a sign above the entrance tunnel. What does it say?
6. Has Halifax ever played in the First Division?

QUIZ 440

1. Which of these teams has appeared in more FA Cup semi-finals than any other - Everton, Liverpool or Manchester United?
2. Which striker is known as 'Aldo'?
3. For which European country did Lubanski star in the 1970s?
4. After having been pulled down by Peter Shilton, who got up to score the penalty which gave Wales their first-ever Wembley victory in 1977?
5. Which two clubs have been described in recent seasons as Scotland's 'New Firm'?
6. What have Brian Clough, Tommy Docherty and Colin Addison in common?

QUIZ 441

1. Which team won the first Wembley Cup Final, defeating West Ham 2-0 in 1923?
2. Who was the young Luton winger who made his debut for Northern Ireland in April 1988, after they had been involved in a tug-of-war with England for his services?
3. Name either of the young Sampdoria strikers who scored for Italy in the European Championships of June 1988.
4. Whom did Alf Ramsey succeed as England team manager?
5. How did 1974 World Cup hero Jurgen Sparwasser tarnish his reputation with East German fans in 1988?
6. Who was both the Football Writers' and PFA Player of the Year for 1987-88?

QUIZ 442

1. What happened to 1936-37 League Champions Manchester City in the following season?
2. Liam Brady began his Football League career with which club?
3. Which former Liverpool and England midfielder joined the Spaniards Athletico Osasuna in September 1987?
4. Was striker Charlie George ever capped by England?
5. Bill Lambton was appointed manager of Scunthorpe in April 1959. For how long did he stay in the job?
6. Who was the first Scotsman to be involved in a £1 million transfer deal?

QUIZ 443

1. Has a Scottish club ever contested an FA Cup Final?
2. Name either of the Arsenal players sent home from the club's 1977 Australian tour for misbehaviour.
3. Who finished as the Spanish League's top goalscorer in four consecutive seasons from 1985 to 1988?
4. Who scored twice for England in the 1966 World Cup semi-final with Portugal?
5. In the 1970s, Birmingham wore their blue and white colours in the same style of jersey as which top European club?
6. Which former Newcastle player was instrumental in bringing Mirandinha to Tyneside in 1987?

QUIZ 444

1. Name the Spurs star whose unfortunate own goal decided the 1987 FA Cup Final.
2. What was the first name of John Charles' brother who was also a Welsh international?
3. From which Northern Rhine port do the 1988 UEFA Cup winners hail?
4. For which country did Andranik Eskandarian score in the 1978 World Cup?
5. Which team are known as 'The O's'?
6. Which two England stars were convicted of 'Breach of the Peace' during a Rangers-Celtic match in October 1987?

QUIZ 445

1. The two clubs which have been drawn together most often in FA Cup history needed four games to settle their third round tie in January 1988 - can you name them?
2. Who was the West Bromwich Albion striker known as 'Bomber'?
3. Which veteran European goalkeeper holds the record for the longest unbeaten spell in international matches?
4. Which successful manager was the first player to be capped for England at all levels?
5. What does Northampton Town's pitch become during the summer months?
6. How many yards should the defending team be from the ball at a free-kick?

QUIZ 446

1. Who replaced Don Revie as Leeds manager in 1974?
2. Which Northern Ireland international kept goal for Celtic in the 1988 Scottish Cup Final, leaving shortly afterwards to join West Ham?
3. Who, in 1983-84, became the first Briton to win the Golden Boot award as Europe's leading goalscorer?
4. Who is Scotland's top World Cup goalscorer of all-time?
5. In 1987, which club became the first in Scotland to install an artificial pitch?
6. Why is Crystal Palace FC so called?

QUIZ 447

1. Which Arsenal player missed a penalty in the 1988 Littlewoods Cup Final?
2. Who, in 1983, when moving from Clyde to Chelsea, became the first player to have his transfer fee set by an international tribunal?
3. Who was the German World Cup star banned for a time over his allegations of drug-taking in the Bundesliga?
4. Which national side did German manager Sepp Piontek take to the final stages of three major championships during the 1980s?
5. During 1988-89, which club had the smallest ground capacity in the Football League?
6. Colo Colo have been fifteen-times champions of which South American country?

QUIZ 448

1. Name the former Everton and Manchester City striker who became manager of Oldham in July 1982.
2. Who is the ex-Leicester centre-half who followed his manager Graham Taylor from Watford to Aston Villa in June 1987?
3. What is the name of Karl-Heinz Rummenigge's younger brother who succeeded him as a star in the Bayern Munich side before leaving for Borussia Dortmund in the summer of 1988?
4. Who were the beaten semi-finalists in the 1988 European Championships?
5. In which colour of strip does Peterborough United play?
6. In which country does the team Portuguesa play?

QUIZ 449

1. Who succeeded Matt Busby as Manchester United boss?
2. Name the defender who was signed by Middlesbrough during 1988-89, despite having a dozen sendings-off to his 'credit'.
3. Which Italian club bought Joe Jordan from Manchester United in 1981?
4. Ronnie Hellstrom was a World Cup goalkeeper for which country?
5. What did Sammy McIlroy once say about his left foot?
6. How many Celtic players were officially sent off in the 1967 World Club Championship decider?

QUIZ 450

1. Who headed Wimbledon's winning goal in the 1988 FA Cup Final?
2. Which Midlands club signed former Rangers winger Ted McMinn from Spanish League team Seville in 1988?
3. Ossie Ardiles left Spurs in 1982 to play one season for which continental club?
4. Which country will host the 1992 European Championship Finals?
5. In 'Till Death Us Do Part', which team did Alf Garnet support?
6. What is the name given to the the North & Central American and Caribbean confederation of FIFA member nations?

QUIZ 451

1. Who was the last player to score with a penalty in the FA Cup Final?
2. For which country was Don Givens an internationalist?
3. Northern Ireland international Gerry Armstrong played with which Spanish club from 1983 to 1985?
4. Has a European nation ever won the World Cup outside of its own continent?
5. Name either of the Scottish First Division teams known as 'The Jags'.
6. Why is the fourth Thursday in March significant for Football League managers?

QUIZ 452

1. Which captain missed the 1983 FA Cup Final through suspension but returned for the replay in which his side lost 4-0?
2. Which veteran Football League goalkeeper is known as 'Budgie'?
3. Which was Liam Brady's first Italian League club?
4. Who skippered England in the 1982 World Cup in the absence of Kevin Keegan?
5. What is the name of Bradford City's ground where the disastrous fire of 1985 occurred?
6. Name Aston Villa's two mangers in the 1986-87 season.

QUIZ 453

1. Which Liverpool defender admitted that his trip on John O'Hare in the 1978 League Cup Final was a 'professional foul' and thus incurred the wrath of the soccer authorities?
2. For which country did goalkeeper Tony Millington play?
3. Which European team paid £900,000 to West Bromwich Albion for Laurie Cunningham in June 1979?
4. Describe Portugal's national strip?
5. At which famous London stadium did QPR play their home matches in 1962-63?
6. Who was the 1989 Footballer of the Year?

QUIZ 454

1. Where was the tragedy-hit 1989 FA Cup semi-final between Liverpool and Nottingham Forest eventually played?
2. From which club did Liverpool sign Graeme Souness in 1978?
3. For which striker did AS Roma pay over £2.5 million to Werder Bremen in the summer of 1987?
4. After Scotland had beaten England 5-1 at Wembley in 1928, what name was given to the Scots forward-line?
5. Why could Spurs not play their opening home game of the 1988-89 season?
6. Which was the last trophy won by Ipswich Town?

QUIZ 455

1. Which striker netted the two goals which won the 1988 Scottish Cup for Celtic?
2. Which feature was common to Liverpool players Steve Heighway, David Johnson and Terry McDermott?
3. Who was the Welsh international forward who won a UEFA Cup medal with PSV Eindhoven in 1978?
4. Which top star was sent off in the Brazil-Argentina World Cup match of 1982?
5. Who plays at Filbert Street?
6. What name links the 1989 managers of Aberdeen, Newcastle and Sunderland?

QUIZ 456

1. Arsenal beat Manchester United 2-1 at Villa Park in October 1988 - in which competition?
2. Who is the former Nottingham Forest and Scotland winger who played for Great Britain in the 1989 Veterans World Cup in Brazil?
3. For which Italian side have Liam Brady, Trevor Francis and Graeme Souness all played?
4. What was the name of the trainer of England's 1966 World Cup squad?
5. According to their record, which football strip did the group, 'Half-man, Half-biscuit' want for Christmas?
6. Who was sacked as Chelsea boss in March 1988?

QUIZ 457

1. Which was the last team to win the Football League Championship on goal average?
2. Who won an FA Cup winners medal with Spurs in 1967, but was a Wembley loser with Fulham in 1975?
3. Name the full-back signed by Southampton from Partizan Belgrade in 1978.
4. Which national team has the letters *CCCP* on its jersey?
5. In the comic *Scorcher*, for which team did 'Bobby of the Blues' play?
6. What title do Barclays bestow on the outstanding young player of each month?

QUIZ 458

1. In August 1987, which was the first club to visit Scarborough for a Football League match?
2. Alex MacDonald, later to boss Hearts, won a European Cup-Winners Cup medal in 1972 with which club?
3. Name the Swedish international striker who joined Benfica from Malmo in August 1987.
4. Tele Santana managed which country in the 1986 World Cup?
5. What was the title of BBC's breakfast-time programme which showed highlights of the previous night's matches during the 1970 World Cup?
6. In 1989, which team won the 'Double' in the Irish Republic?

QUIZ 459

1. Which is the only ground other than Wembley to have staged a post-war FA Cup Final?
2. Ray Hankin was top League goalscorer at which club in the 1977-78 First Division?
3. Why did QPR play their 1984 UEFA Cup matches at Highbury?
4. Which member of Brazil's all-conquering 1970 side had to quit football because of eye trouble?
5. What is the nickname of both Crewe Alexandra and Lokomotiv Leipzig?
6. Which former Liverpool and Eire star became boss of Oxford United in April 1988?

QUIZ 460

1. Who succeeded Keith Burkinshaw as Tottenham boss in 1984?
2. Which Merseyside midfielder is known as 'Macca'?
3. Who is the *spielfuhrer* in a German team?
4. Which 1982 World Cup team were known to their fans as the 'Untameable Lions'?
5. Which member of England's famous 1966 team now works as an undertaker?
6. Who was voted the PFA's Young Player of the Year for 1988-89?

QUIZ 461

1. Which former League club was expelled from the GM Vauxhall Conference in 1989?
2. Which England manager captained Arsenal to two League Championships and an FA Cup victory?
3. From which continental club did Celtic sign striker Mark McGhee in 1985?
4. Which team beat Zaire 9-0 in the 1974 World Cup?
5. *True Blue* is the autobiography of which Scottish international winger?
6. Who was the last senior player to score a hat-trick in a Wembley cup final? (he did do in March 1986)

QUIZ 462

1. Which was the last London team other than Arsenal to win the First Division?
2. From which club did QPR sign international defender Paul Parker?
3. Jesus Gil is the outspoken president of which European club?
4. Who scored a hat-trick for England in their 9-3 win over Scotland in 1961?
5. To which political leader did Ruud Gullit dedicate his 1987 European Footballer of the Year award?
6. With which Scottish club did Chelsea supremo Ken Bates become connected in 1986?

QUIZ 463

1. Which Scottish First Division club held Rangers to a draw in the 1989 Scottish Cup semi-final before going down 4-0 in the replay?
2. From which club did Everton sign striker Bob Latchford for £350,000 in 1974?
3. 1987 Golden Boot winner Rodion Camataru hit 44 goals that year, for which Rumanian club?
4. Which two home nations reached the 1982 World Cup from the same qualifying section?
5. Who was 'ten years ahead of his time' according to Alf Ramsey?
6. Which club won the 1989 Welsh Cup?

QUIZ 464

1. Which team were Second Division Champions in 1988-89?
2. At which club did Liverpool veteran Ian Callaghan finish his League career?
3. Which French club bought Jesper Olsen from Manchester United for £650,000 in November 1988?
4. Which South American country walloped Scotland 7-0 in the 1954 World Cup?
5. Which club employs a boatman to retrieve lost balls from the nearby River Severn?
6. Who won the 1988-89 GM Vauxhall Conference title?

QUIZ 465

1. Name the manager who lead Manchester City to promotion in 1989.
2. Former Leeds United striker Carl Harris won 24 caps for which country?
3. Who is the Swedish international who played for Rangers from 1982 to 1985?
4. Name the Danish striker who hit a hat-trick in the 6-1 World Cup demolition of Uruguay in 1986.
5. Who are 'The Quakers'?
6. Which organisation is Scotsman William McGregor credited with founding?

--------- **QUIZ 466** ---------

1. Which current Second Division side were Division One runners-up in 1981 and 1982?
2. Who kept goal for Nottingham Forest in two Wembley cup finals during 1989?
3. Which country had representatives in all three European tournament finals in 1989?
4. Which of these countries has never beaten England in a full international - Denmark, Norway or East Germany?
5. In the TV series 'Scully', which famous footballer kept appearing in the youngster's dreams?
6. In April 1988, which club sacked manager Alex Smith less than a year after he had steered them to Scottish Cup success?

--------- **QUIZ 467** ---------

1. Which was the last team besides Celtic or Rangers to win the Scottish 'Double'?
2. Who was 'Wee Alex' who played for Raith Rovers, Preston and later Arsenal where he became a world-famous star of the 1930s?
3. Name the former Real Madrid full-back and captain who is Spain's most capped player.
4. Who was the Holland substitute whose late headed goal took the 1978 World Cup Final into extra-time?
5. What did Watford forward Cliff Holton do on both 15 and 16 April 1960?
6. Name the veteran Scottish international who, at 41, was the Football League's oldest player in 1988-89.

--------- **QUIZ 468** ---------

1. Which Second Division team sent Spurs crashing from the 1989 FA Cup?
2. Name the Israeli international who joined QPR from Cologne in 1987.
3. Which veteran Italian striker is known as 'The Big Pin'?
4. Who were the top scorers in the qualifying groups for the 1988 European Championships?
5. Who is the Scottish international once voted 'The man I would most like to go out with' by Samantha Fox?
6. Name the ex-Spurs captain who managed Brentford to the 1989 FA Cup quarter-finals.

QUIZ 469

1. Which founder member club narrowly avoided automatic expulsion from the League by winning its last match at home to Orient in May 1987?
2. Who, in 1988, became the first goalkeeper to captain an FA Cup-winning side at Wembley?
3. Which leading Swedish club shares the Ullevi Stadium with IFK Gothenburg?
4. 1987 South American Footballer of the Year Carlos Valderrama stars in midfield for which national side?
5. Which experienced Football League defender is known as 'Fozzie'?
6. Which team won a 'Battle of Britain' to take the Dubai Super Cup in April 1989?

QUIZ 470

1. When Liverpool stayed undefeated for 29 League games from the start of the 1987-88 season, they equalled the record of which famous side of the 1970s?
2. Name the crop-haired Wolves striker who finished 1988-89 as the Football League's top goalscorer for the second consecutive season.
3. In which country's league did World Cup veterans Giancarlo Antognoni, Marco Tardelli and Karl-Heinz Rummenigge all play during 1988-89?
4. Which country had a World Cup goalkeeper called Gilmar?
5. Which League club plays its home matches in Cleethorpes?
6. Has Wembley ever staged a Football League match?

QUIZ 471

1. In 1908, after defeating QPR 4-0, Manchester United became the first winners of which trophy?
2. Who is the former Wolves, Arsenal and Ipswich striker who helped Derry City win the First Division of the 1987 League of Ireland?
3. For which club did Gheorghe Hagi score six European Cup goals in 1988-89?
4. Former Blackpool and Burnley goalkeeper Tony Waiters managed which national team in the 1986 World Cup?
5. Which top Scottish team plays in an all-red outfit?
6. Who was sacked as Birmingham manager in May 1987?

QUIZ 472

1. Who holds the record for the highest career total of Football League goals?
2. Jim Herriot, who kept goal for Birmingham, was an international for which country?
3. Who are the 'Rossoneri'?
4. Which of these players won the most England caps - Emlyn Hughes, Mick Mills or Stanley Matthews?
5. What have the cities of Bristol, Nottingham, Manchester, Stoke and Sheffield in common?
6. Who was the Scottish Footballer of the Year for 1989?

QUIZ 473

1. In 1982-83, which team, in their first-ever season in Division One, finished as runners-up to Liverpool?
2. Who was the West Bromwich Albion player, once sent off for kicking the referee on the backside?
3. Dutch international 'keeper Hans Van Breukelen once played for which Football League club?
4. Who is generally considered to have been the greatest footballer never to have played in the final stages of the World Cup?
5. What was unusual about Liverpool's 1988 Cup Final record?
6. Which club set up a new attendance record for the Vauxhall Conference when 9,432 people watched them play Wycombe in the final game of the 1987-88 season?

QUIZ 474

1. Name the beaten semi-finalists in the 1988-89 Littlewoods Cup.
2. Ian Moore of Nottingham Forest and Manchester United was an international cap for which country?
3. Which team defeated Aberdeen in the first round of the 1988-89 UEFA Cup?
4. Which Portuguese player hit four goals against North Korea in the 1966 World Cup?
5. Who was Nobby Stiles' brother-in-law who often played against him in Leeds-Manchester United clashes?
6. Which country has a team called Arab Contractors?

QUIZ 475

1. Who, in 1987-88, became the first player since George Best to score over 20 League goals in a season for Manchester United?
2. Name the skipper of Celtic's Scottish Cup-winning side of 1989.
3. Goalkeeper Uli Stein has a European Cup medal. With which club did he win it?
4. Which key defender missed England's European Championship matches in Germany because of a broken leg injury?
5. Which is the only British senior team with a 'J' in its name?
6. In 1987, which TV personality stepped in to bail Fulham out of financial trouble?

QUIZ 476

1. Which Merseyside team progressed the furthest in the 1988 League Centenary Festival at Wembley?
2. Which Welsh international is known as 'Rats'?
3. Who were the 1989 champions of France?
4. In which city did Northern Ireland beat Spain in the 1982 World Cup?
5. Which footballer was the subject of Don Fardon's 1970 hit record 'Belfast Boy'?
6. Which Scottish club has lost seven consecutive major cup finals since 1981?

QUIZ 477

1. Who skippered Arsenal to Littlewoods Cup success in 1987?
2. Which English international striker was known as 'Attila' during his spell in Italian football?
3. Who is the former West German international boss who steered Galatasary to two consecutive Turkish championships in 1987 and 1988?
4. Who scored England's last Home International Championship goal in the 1-1 draw with Scotland in 1984?
5. In which aspect of stadium construction did Scunthorpe United lead the rest of Britain in 1958?
6. Who refereed the 1989 FA Cup Final?

QUIZ 478

1. Which team knocked out holders Wimbledon from the 1989 FA Cup?
2. For which club did Tony Agana and Brian Deane score a combined total of 60 goals during 1988-89?
3. Surinam-born Stanley Menzo kept goal for which club in 1987 and 1988 European finals?
4. Who were England's only goalscorers in the 1988 European Championship Finals?
5. Which player made fifteen Wembley appearances with Liverpool from 1977 to 1987?
6. Who is the former Scotland centre-half who managed Airdrie from 1987 to 1989?

QUIZ 479

1. Which manager led both Doncaster Rovers and Grimsby Town to the Fourth Division Championship?
2. In the 1987-88 season, who was the only First Division goalkeeper to keep two clean sheets in League matches against Liverpool?
3. Who was the first Englishman to manage a European Cup-winning side?
4. What is the nationality of FIFA president Joao Havelange?
5. Which First Division club's 1988-89 teamsheet included the name of a former American President?
6. Who replaced Dave Bassett as Watford manager?

QUIZ 480

1. Name any of the three players who each hit a double in the thrilling 1989 Simod Cup Final.
2. Who was the leading goalscorer of Arsenal's 1989 Championship team?
3. Why is home advantage not a significant factor in the Maltese Premier Division?
4. What number did hat-trick hero Geoff Hurst wear in the 1966 World Cup?
5. What was new about TV coverage of the 1968 FA Cup Final?
6. In 1988, which club became the first in modern times to lose its First Division status as a result of the play-offs?

─────────────── **QUIZ 481** ───────────────

1. During 1987, which Third Division club notched 8-1 and 10-0 victories in consecutive weeks?
2. Name the midfielder who first achieved notoriety after 'getting to grips' with Paul Gascoigne during a 1988 League match between Wimbledon and Newcastle.
3. Which top European midfield star was born in France's old African colony of Mali?
4. Has Brazil ever lost a World Cup Final?
5. Which sport did the fathers of both Emlyn Hughes and Peter Barnes play?
6. Which team won the 1988 Guinness Soccer Six tournament in Manchester?

─────────────── **QUIZ 482** ───────────────

1. What did Aldershot, Queen of the South and Stenhousemuir all do in 1989?
2. Which First Division team did Mickey Phelan captain during 1988-89?
3. At which German club did Danish striker Flemming Povlsen join his fellow countryman Morten Olsen in 1987?
4. Who was Scotland's top scorer in the 1974 World Cup in Germany?
5. Who is the forward who was born in Huddersfield, holds a degree in Russian and plays for the Republic of Ireland?
6. Name any one of the three Football League clubs which have never been relegated.

─────────────── **QUIZ 483** ───────────────

1. Name the manager who led Wimbeldon to FA Cup glory in 1988.
2. From which team did Liverpool sign Phil Neal in 1974?
3. Name either of the two leading European goalkeepers who each played in one half for the Rest of the World against the Football League in August 1987.
4. After 1962, when did England next successfully negotiate the World Cup qualifying competition?
5. How did Wimbeldon surprise many people when they arrived at White Hart Lane for the 1988 FA Cup semi-final?
6. According to the Laws of the Game, what is the minimum number of players a team must have for a match to continue?

QUIZ 484

1. In November 1960, who became the youngest player to have scored 100 League goals when he netted for Chelsea against Manchester City?
2. Name the midfielder who joined Celtic from Hearts for £550,000 in June 1989.
3. Which Rangers striker was joint top goalscorer in the 1988 European Cup competition?
4. In which colour of shirt does Colombia play?
5. Which West Country team are nicknamed 'The Pirates'?
6. What are Delta, Match and Multiplex?

QUIZ 485

1. Who scored the only goal of the 1989 Norwich-Everton FA Cup semi-final?
2. Which former Sheffield Wednesday team-mates opposed each other in the 1989 Scottish Cup Final?
3. Italian international striker Roberto Bettega notched many valuable goals for which club side?
4. Who were Holland's goalscorers in their 1988 European Championship Final victory over the Soviet Union?
5. Who sang a solo part in Spurs' 1981 Cup Final record made with Chas and Dave?
6. Which Ian Rush/Liverpool record did Arsenal end when they defeated them in the 1987 Littlewoods Cup Final?

QUIZ 486

1. Who was Luton's two-goal hero in the 1988 Littlewoods Cup Final?
2. Name either of the clubs for which England international Martin Dobson played First Division soccer in the 1970s.
3. Which country had half of its top division's clubs involved in European competitions during 1988-89?
4. For which country did Michel star in 1988-89 World Cup qualifying games?
5. What is the nickname of Blackpool FC?
6. Which manager lead Chelsea to the 1989 Division Two Championship?

QUIZ 487

1. Name any of the three Midlands clubs which lost their Division Two place in 1989.
2. Who was the former Bradford, Birmingham, Sheffield United, Norwich and Wales star who tragically died after a five-a-side game in April 1987?
3. Name the veteran Belgian international full-back who skippered PSV Eindhoven's highly successful team of 1987-88.
4. Name the Nottingham Forest defender who won his first England cap against Brazil in May 1987.
5. Who appeared in the 1988 Cup Final with a brand new set of front teeth?
6. At which major English club did Doug Ellis begin his third stint as chairman in December 1982?

QUIZ 488

1. Whose miss in the penalty shoot-out cost Aberdeen the 1987-88 Skol Cup Final?
2. At which club did striker Garth Crooks begin his career?
3. Which European country attracts the highest average crowds to its league matches?
4. Which of the home countries made the quarter-finals of the 1958 World Cup in Sweden?
5. Which TV presenter once said 'There'll be more football in a moment, but first we've got the highlights of the Scottish League Cup Final'?
6. What was particularly impressive about Arsenal's 1971 FA Cup win?

QUIZ 489

1. Who was West Ham's unused substitute for the 1975 FA Cup Final?
2. For which Second Division club did veteran striker Keith Edwards notch 30 goals during 1988-89?
3. What are the names of the Hoeness brothers who have both played for Bayern Munich and West Germany?
4. Who was the Celtic forward who, in 1977, scored a goal for Scotland without having kicked a ball in international football?
5. Which club had England's first all-seater stadium?
6. Who received the 1989 Simod Cup on behalf of Nottingham Forest?

QUIZ 490

1. Which player holds the record for appearances in Football League matches?
2. Name Rangers' young Scottish international midfielder who sustained a serious leg injury during the league match at Aberdeen in October 1988.
3. Who was the star French centre-forward who played in three European Cup Finals for Real Madrid?
4. Which Liverpool star scored the only goal of the England v Republic of Ireland clash in the 1988 European Championships?
5. Which electronics company had its name on the shirts of both Arsenal and Aberdeen during 1989?
6. In January 1987, which team failed to turn up at Anfield for an FA Cup replay?

QUIZ 491

1. Which is the only major domestic competition which Brian Clough has never won as a manager?
2. Name the former Albion Rovers and Morton striker who hit 18 goals for Middlesbrough in 1988-89.
3. Who were the 1989 champions of Greece?
4. By May 1989, England had gone five years undefeated at Wembley. Which country won there back in June 1984?
5. What colour of boots did England star Alan Ball favour?
6. Which two England internationalists kept goal for Rangers during the 1987-88 season?

QUIZ 492

1. How many Englishmen were in the Rangers team which beat Hearts 4-0 to clinch the Scottish Championship in April 1989?
2. In March 1989, which QPR player was controversially fined by manager Trevor Francis for missing a match to attend the birth of his first child?
3. Which two Englishmen helped Monaco win the 1988 French League?
4. Which England star was sent off in a 1973 World Cup tie against Poland in Chorzow?
5. Who wrote the book *Going Great Guns*?
6. Name the manager who steered Wolves to the Third and Fourth Division Championships in the late 1980s.

QUIZ 493

1. Which side has won ten of the last twelve Irish League Championships?
2. The son of a 1966 World Cup hero made his League debut in March 1985 when he played for Leeds United at Middlesbrough. Can you name him and his father?
3. Where was the 1989 European Cup Final played?
4. Name the Brazilian striker, who was snapped up by PSV Eindhoven after finishing as seven-goal top scorer in the Seoul Olympics.
5. Which Scottish side plays its home matches in a major athletics stadium?
6. Of which league were Merthyr Tydfil the 1989 champions?

QUIZ 494

1. Name the Welsh international goalkeeper who made a vital penalty save and was voted Man of the Match in Luton's 1988 Littlewoods Cup Final victory.
2. Which current First Division manager scored all four goals in Aston Villa's 2-2 draw at Leicester in March 1976?
3. Which childhood friend of Ruud Gullit's played alongside him for AC Milan and Holland during 1988-89?
4. Name the young central defender who made his England debut against Hungary in Budapest in April 1988.
5. Why was Swiss club Xamax Neuchatel fined £6500 by UEFA in October 1988?
6. Which top London side is named after a Shakespearian character?

QUIZ 495

1. Which team finished bottom of Division Four in 1989, thus ending its 68-year membership of the Football League?
2. In 1971, which Arsenal player secured a winner's medal at Wembley, at his fifth attempt?
3. What nationality is Anderlecht striker Arnor Gudjohnsen?
4. Which country won the 1987 South American championship with a bruising 1-0 victory over Chile in Buenos Aires?
5. Which Scottish League club folded in 1967?
6. Which Yorkshire club has been managed in recent seasons by Malcolm Macdonald and Eoin Hand?

QUIZ 496

1. Who won the 1988 FA Charity Shield?
2. Which Welsh international striker did Charlton sign from Port Vale for £300,000 in September 1987?
3. Name the Dutch manager who was replaced by John Toshack at Real Madrid during 1989.
4. Which European national team has not won a competitive match since beating Turkey 2-0 in October 1972?
5. What is unusual about the way that the players get from the dressing-room to the pitch in the Parkstadion, Gelsenkirchen?
6. If a cup final has ended in a draw after ninety minutes play, how long should the interval between normal and extra-time be?

QUIZ 497

1. Which was the last club other than Liverpool to retain the Football League Championship?
2. Joe Miller, Billy Stark and Mark McGhee, team-mates in Celtic's 1988 'Double' side, have all played for which other major Scottish club?
3. Which club took the 1989 Belgian League title?
4. Name either of England's goalscorers in their 2-0 Hampden victory over Scotland in May 1989.
5. Which company did Watford not stick with for their 1988-89 shirt sponsorship?
6. May defenders ever be less than 10 yards from the ball at a free-kick?

QUIZ 498

1. Name the Scottish manager who, in 1988-89, lead Millwall in their first-ever season in Division One.
2. Which goalkeeper made his long-awaited England debut against Saudi Arabia in November 1988?
3. Name the Uruguayan international signed by Racing Club of Paris after he impressed during the 1986 World Cup.
4. Who took charge of the Welsh national team in April 1988?
5. Which sportswear company supplied the 1988-89 kits for Coventry, Aston Villa, Real Madrid and Wales?
6. Why could 1988 Simod Cup winners Reading not defend the trophy in the following season's competition?

QUIZ 499

1. Which two clubs contested the Final of the Football League Centenary Festival at Wembley in April 1988?
2. What age was Peter Shilton on 18 September 1989?
3. Which club won the 1989 Portuguese Championship?
4. Against which country did Scotland score their first-ever victory in the World Cup Finals?
5. Who was known as *Charlie Sciampagna* (Champagne Charlie) by fans of Sampdoria?
6. Name the former Arsenal manager who was coach to Wimbledon's victorious 1988 FA Cup team.

QUIZ 500

1. Which former Scotland captain led Middlesbrough from Third Division to First in the late 1980s?
2. Name the veteran striker who captained the Republic of Ireland in the 1988 European Championships.
3. In 1988, PSV became the third club to win the European Cup in the same season as its own national league and cup. Can you name either of the other two clubs which have achieved this?
4. What did Under-21 internationals replace?
5. Which club moved from The Old Show Ground to Glanford Park in 1988?
6. What was the score in the Football League's Centenary match against the Rest of the World in August 1987?

QUIZ 1
1. Billy Bonds
2. Trevor Francis
3. Eindhoven
4. Bobby Moore
5. Yellow shirts, navy blue shorts
6. 8 feet

QUIZ 2
1. Michael Thomas
2. Clyde Best
3. The European Cup-Winners Cup
4. Mario Kempes
5. Southampton
6. Don Revie

QUIZ 3
1. Ian Ferguson
2. Clive and Paul Allen
3. Hibernian
4. John Barnes
5. Roker Park
6. Leeds United

QUIZ 4
1. Kenny Sansom
2. Alan McInally
3. Real Madrid
4. Peter Shilton
5. 'You'll Never Walk Alone'
6. England's World Cup success of 1966

QUIZ 5
1. Roy Aitken
2. Leicester, Stoke, Nottingham Forest, Southampton and Derby
3. Ajax (of Amsterdam)
4. Gordon McQueen
5. Glenn Hoddle's
6. Sir Stanley Rous

QUIZ 6
1. Coventry City
2. Charlton
3. Anderlecht
4. Monterrey
5. 'Quizball'
6. Yeovil Town

QUIZ 7
1. Tony Barton
2. David Narey
3. Napoli
4. Wales
5. Liam Brady
6. Torino

QUIZ 8
1. Stuart McCall
2. Avi Cohen
3. Barcelona
4. Alf Ramsey
5. Arsenal
6. The Spanish Cup, in March 1988

QUIZ 9
1. The Football League Cup
2. Ian Hutchinson
3. Alan Kennedy's
4. East Germany
5. Swansea
6. Albion Rovers and Raith Rovers

QUIZ 10
1. Celtic
2. Pat Jennings
3. Reims
4. Trevor Brooking and Kevin Keegan
5. West Ham
6. 22

QUIZ 11
1. Norwich City
2. Erik Thorstvedt
3. The Soviet Union
4. Bobby Charlton
5. Kevin Keegan
6. The 'away' team

QUIZ 12
1. Four – Aberdeen, Celtic, Dundee United and Rangers
2. West Ham
3. Ferenc Puskas
4. Gordon Strachan
5. An artificial pitch
6. May

QUIZ 13
1. Birmingham City
2. Reading
3. Blue and white
4. Malcolm Macdonald
5. Birkenhead
6. Graham Taylor

QUIZ 14
1. Tottenham Hotspur, in 1951
2. 1977
3. 1 – 0
4. Yugoslavia
5. Vicarage Road
6. Jack Charlton

QUIZ 15
1. Leicester City
2. Peter Davenport
3. Dundee
4. Geoff Hurst
5. Queen's Park Rangers
6. 100 yards

QUIZ 16
1. Norwich City
2. Paris St Germain
3. Videoton
4. 13-0 to England
5. Thatchem United
6. Liverpool

QUIZ 17
1. Blackpool
2. Gerry Armstrong. He is a Northern Ireland international – the others have been capped for the Republic.
3. Inter-Milan
4. Zaire
5. Nelli Kim
6. 12 yards

QUIZ 18
1. Southampton
2. West Ham
3. John Hewitt
4. 1984
5. Airdrieonians
6. Blackpool

QUIZ 19
1. Bill Shankly, famous Liverpool manager
2. Aston Villa
3. Partizan Belgrade
4. Canada and Iraq
5. Jasper Carrott
6. Bell's Whisky

QUIZ 20
1. The Anglo-Italian Cup in 1971
2. Alex Ferguson
3. The Fairs Cup
4. Paul Mariner
5. Linfield
6. Swansea

QUIZ 21
1. Bolton Wanderers
2. Eire
3. Steve Chalmers
4. Richard Gough
5. Wimbledon

6. Five (Any two may be used)

QUIZ 22
1. Sheffield Wednesday
2. West Ham
3. Wembley
4. Tostao
5. White
6. Bob Lord

QUIZ 23
1. Bournemouth
2. Martin Peters
3. Ruud Gullit
4. Sweden
5. 'The Red Devils'
6. Billy Bingham

QUIZ 24
1. Jock Wallace
2. Steve Daley
3. The Heysel Stadium in Brussels
4. Emlyn Hughes
5. Preben Elkjaer
6. Gary Lineker

QUIZ 25
1. Notts County
2. Brighton and Portsmouth
3. Manchester (United as holders, City as League Champions)
4. Danny McGrain
5. Jim McLean of Dundee United
6. Red

QUIZ 26
1. Ian Rush
2. England
3. Hearts
4. Portugal
5. Northern Ireland
6. Blackburn Rovers

QUIZ 27
1. Yes
2. Kevin Beattie
3. AC Milan
4. Bryan Robson, for England against France
5. Today
6. Doncaster Rovers

QUIZ 28
1. Bristol City
2. John McGovern
3. The Union of European Football Associations

4. Graeme Souness
5. Race
6. Lytham St Annes

QUIZ 29
1. Chris Nicholl
2. Brian Clough
3. Leeds United
4. Birmingham City
5. 'I'm Forever Blowing Bubbles'
6. Detroit Express

QUIZ 30
1. Aston Villa in 1981
2. Manchester City
3. Feyenoord
4. Peru's (Ramon Quiroga)
5. No.10
6. The Highland League

QUIZ 31
1. Ian Redford
2. Queen's Park Rangers
3. Panathinaikos
4. Don Masson
5. White Hart Lane
6. Luton Town

QUIZ 32
1. Charlton
2. Trevor Steven
3. Dukla Prague
4. Guy Thys
5. Armando
6. Argentinos Juniors, Boca Juniors, Barcelona

QUIZ 33
1. Wolves
2. Gordon Durie
3. Borussia Moenchengladbach
4. Bobby Charlton
5. Celtic Park (also known as Parkhead)
6. The Texaco Cup

QUIZ 34
1. Geoff Hurst
2. Pierce
3. Ajax Amsterdam
4. Pele
5. Charlie Nicholas
6. Edson Arantes do Nascimento

QUIZ 35
1. Ron Harris
2. Celtic

3. Atletico Madrid
4. Michel Platini
5. He is a dentist
6. The League Champions and FA Cup Holders

QUIZ 36
1. Manchester City
2. QPR
3. Bayern Munich
4. Allan Clarke
5. Manchester City
6. He was a referee

QUIZ 37
1. Chesterfield
2. Chelsea
3. Andy Gray
4. Brazil
5. He refused to clean them until Morocco were knocked out
6. Chicago Sting

QUIZ 38
1. They all went to a replay
2. Dai Davies
3. Jimmy Armfield
4. Kenny Dalglish
5. Clocks
6. In the centre circle

QUIZ 39
1. Coventry City
2. Alan Brazil
3. St Etienne's
4. Helmut Haller
5. Belle Vue, Doncaster
6. Kidderminster Harriers

QUIZ 40
1. Crystal Palace
2. Kevin Drinkell
3. Charlie George
4. Haiti
5. Green, black and white
6. 92

QUIZ 41
1. Roy McFarland
2. Kenny Dalglish
3. Cyprus
4. Jan Jongbloed
5. Archie Macpherson
6. The HFS Loans Northern Premier League

QUIZ 42
1. Everton
2. Cyrille Regis

3. Rome
4. Holland
5. Jack Charlton
6. Two, direct and indirect

QUIZ 43
1. Fulham
2. Allan Evans
3. Barcelona
4. Australia
5. 'World Cup Willie'
6. Phil Neal

QUIZ 44
1. Orient
2. David Fairclough
3. Terry McDermott
4. Gerry Armstrong
5. Portman Road
6. Bobby Moore

QUIZ 45
1. Richard Money
2. Wolves
3. FC Bruges
4. 0 - 0
5. Joe
6. 22 – The teams were numbered 1
   - 11 (Everton) and 12-22 (Man
   City)

QUIZ 46
1. Newcastle
2. Manchester City
3. Ferencvaros
4. Bilbao
5. Hamilton Accies
6. Ted Croker

QUIZ 47
1. Hartlepool
2. Tottenham
3. Eindhoven
4. Cyprus
5. Jimmy Greaves'
6. Three (Assuming that their opponents have missed their first three)

QUIZ 48
1. 1972
2. John Fashanu
3. Czechoslovakia
4. West Germany
5. Odsal Stadium
6. Fine-Fare

QUIZ 49
1. Hull City
2. Gary Shaw

3. Malmo of Sweden
4. Denis Law
5. Castleburn
6. No, the law says the length must
   always exceed the breadth

QUIZ 50
1. Willie Miller
2. Ian Wilson
3. Bobby Houghton
4. Holland and West Germany
5. 'Give us a Goal'
6. Manchester City

QUIZ 51
1. Leeds United
2. West Ham
3. Fiorentina
4. Mexico
5. Emlyn Hughes
6. LA Aztecs

QUIZ 52
1. 10-0
2. Wales
3. Kevin Keegan
4. Billy Bremner
5. Blue and white halves
6. 1975-76

QUIZ 53
1. Peter Lorimer
2. Jim Cumbes
3. Blue and white
4. Eusebio of Portugal
5. Brighton
6. Sheffield

QUIZ 54
1. Coventry City
2. Alan Ball
3. CSKA Sofia
4. Ray Wilkins
5. Bristol City
6. Jack Charlton

QUIZ 55
1. Bryan Hamilton
2. Southampton
3. Aberdeen
4. Tony Adams
5. Steve Cram
6. 10 yards

QUIZ 56
1. Leicester City
2. Brian Flynn

3. Galatasaray
4. Mexico
5. Arsenal
6. Bristol City

QUIZ 57
1. Emlyn Hughes
2. Steve Gatting
3. Real Madrid
4. Yellow
5. Belfast
6. Volcano United

QUIZ 58
1. Ian Callaghan
2. AC Milan
3. Graham Roberts
4. South Korea
5. Alex Ferguson
6. Tottenham

QUIZ 59
1. 1962
2. Southampton
3. Peter Withe
4. White and blue
5. ITV's attempt to sign an exclusive deal on coverage of League football. They eventually succeeded in this in 1988
6. No

QUIZ 60
1. Ipswich Town
2. Bruce Grobbelaar
3. White
4. Bulgaria
5. Glenn Hoddle and Chris Waddle
6. Blackburn Rovers

QUIZ 61
1. Manager Bill Nicholson
2. Arthur Albiston
3. Shamrock Rovers
4. Portugal
5. Hearts
6. Toronto

QUIZ 62
1. Manchester City
2. David Giles
3. Six
4. Hungary
5. *Escape to Victory*
6. Antonio Rattin of Argentina

QUIZ 63
1. Tottenham
2. Hibernian

3. Zbigniew Boniek
4. Nat Lofthouse
5. Red
6. The Gola League

QUIZ 64
1. Matt Busby
2. Gary Gillespie
3. Felix Magath
4. Julio Cesar Romero (also known as 'Romerito')
5. Bournemouth
6. Luton Town

QUIZ 65
1. Celtic
2. Mal Donaghy
3. Real Betis
4. Jairzinho
5. Jules Rimet
6. They said it would over crowd their fixtures

QUIZ 66
1. Manchester United
2. Andy Gray
3. The European Cup-Winners Cup
4. Sammy McIlroy
5. Highfield Road, Coventry
6. Derby, Notts County and Stockport

QUIZ 67
1. One
2. Chris Balderstone
3. Bernd Schuster
4. Bobby Moore
5. 'Back Home'
6. 5 minutes

QUIZ 68
1. Middlesbrough
2. Aston Villa
3. Rome
4. Steve Hodge
5. He is a radio commentator
6. Eddie Niedzwiecki

QUIZ 69
1. Millwall
2. Stein
3. Milan
4. England and Wales
5. Watford
6. 64

QUIZ 70
1. Martin Buchan
2. Andy Goram

3. Sweden
4. Frankie Vercauteren
5. Old Trafford
6. Frans Thijssen

QUIZ 71

1. Liverpool
2. None
3. Steaua Bucharest
4. France
5. Rothmans
6. The 'away goals rule'

QUIZ 72

1. Nottingham Forest
2. Alan Gilzean
3. Terry Venables
4. White City
5. Tangerine
6. Fulham

QUIZ 73

1. Orient, which became Leyton Orient again
2. Jim Baxter
3. Belgium
4. Tommy Docherty
5. Anfield
6. War was declared on 3 September 1939 and the season was officially ended, with Lawton the only player to have scored

QUIZ 74

1. Southend United
2. Wales
3. FC Magdeburg
4. 1-1
5. The player's number
6. Chelsea

QUIZ 75

1. John Wile
2. Billy Hamilton
3. Goalkeeper Jimmy Rimmer
4. Honduras
5. Steve Sutton
6. Johnny Carey in 1949

QUIZ 76

1. Malcolm Allison
2. Alan Hansen
3. Bobby Moncur
4. Jim Blyth
5. Sheffield Wednesday
6. 5th

QUIZ 77

1. No
2. Steve Bruce
3. Inter-Milan
4. The Soviet Union
5. Highbury
6. Bournemouth and Boscombe Athletic

QUIZ 78

1. Portsmouth
2. Algeria
3. Nobody – Celtic don't have numbered jerseys!
4. Butragueno
5. A tackle whereby, instead of playing the ball, a player deliberately goes over it into an opponent
6. Telford United

QUIZ 79

1. Queen's Park Rangers
2. Nottingham Forest
3. Eusebio
4. Finland
5. 'The Blaydon Races'
6. Because of the winter shutdown in many countries

QUIZ 80

1. Preston
2. Leeds United
3. Inter-Milan
4. Igor Belanov
5. To watch closed-circuit TV coverage of the match
6. Washington Diplomats

QUIZ 81

1. Reading
2. Trevor Brooking
3. Hamburg
4. Terry Neill
5. Because they were refused permission to play in bare feet!
6. Northern Ireland

QUIZ 82

1. Rotherham United
2. West Bromwich Albion
3. England
4. Pat Jennings
5. Stirling Albion (Their former manager Bob Shankly was related to Liverpool's Bill Shankly)
6. 200,000

QUIZ 83
1. Sheffield United
2. Dundee United
3. Thirteen
4. Ron Greenwood
5. Bill Shankly
6. Sandy Jardine

QUIZ 84
1. Martin Peters
2. Aston Villa
3. Liverpool, at Wembley in 1978
4. North Korea
5. Oxford United
6. Fulham

QUIZ 85
1. Ron Springett
2. Rangers
3. Uli Stielike
4. Keith Newton
5. Chelsea
6. Danny Blanchflower

QUIZ 86
1. Southampton
2. Ipswich
3. Laurie Cunningham
4. France
5. Gillingham
6. 'The Old Firm'

QUIZ 87
1. Norwich City
2. Trevor Hebberd
3. Stan Bowles
4. Joey Jones
5. Zaire
6. The three new member countries of the Common Market (Britain, Denmark and Eire) whose joint team played the six original members in a commemorative match

QUIZ 88
1. Wales
2. Matthew Le Tissier
3. Dundee United
4. Martin Peters
5. Burnley
6. Geoff Hurst

QUIZ 89
1. Swindon Town
2. Manchester City
3. Celtic, in 1967
4. Jack Kelsey
5. The liver-bird
6. Wealdstone

QUIZ 90
1. Eddie Kelly
2. The Republic of Ireland
3. Charlie George
4. Carlos Bilardo
5. Cyril Knowles ('Nice One Cyril')
6. York City

QUIZ 91
1. Keith Burkinshaw
2. Allan Clarke
3. Rangers
4. Nico Claesen
5. A broken goal-post
6. Rangers

QUIZ 92
1. Jimmy Greaves
2. QPR
3. Atletico Madrid
4. Brian Labone
5. Admiral
6. Corner-flags

QUIZ 93
1. Liverpool
2. Newcastle
3. Because the Cup-winners, Spurs, had also won the League and so entered the European Cup
4. Scotland
5. Plymouth Argyle
6. Kevin Keegan

QUIZ 94
1. Celtic
2. Wimbledon
3. Tottenham in 1963
4. The Soviet Union
5. Green shirts with white hoops, green shorts and socks
6. The 'Soccer Bowl'

QUIZ 95
1. John Barnes (now at Liverpool)
2. Leighton James
3. Munich 1860
4. Italy
5. 'Ally's Tartan Army'
6. Northwich Victoria

QUIZ 96
1. 1961
2. Eric Gates
3. Stockholm
4. England and Cameroon
5. Crewe Alexandra
6. Seven

QUIZ 97
1. They have applied for re-election more times (14) than any other club
2. Dickie Guy
3. Barcelona
4. Northern Ireland
5. David Coleman
6. Graeme Souness

QUIZ 98
1. Nobby Stiles
2. Kevin Hird
3. Kenny Dalglish
4. Paul Gascoigne
5. A manager – the team was picked by a committee
6. The Associate Members Cup

QUIZ 99
1. Wolves
2. Ian Gillard
3. Slovan Bratislava
4. Peter Beardsley
5. Kilmarnock
6. Carlisle United

QUIZ 100
1. Aberdeen
2. Liam Brady
3. The USSR
4. Gerd Muller
5. Dana
6. 13

QUIZ 101
1. Nigel Clough
2. Watford
3. Gornik Zabrze
4. Pasadena, California
5. Because, being the time of the Falklands War, they decided their strip was too similar to Argentina's colours
6. Southampton

QUIZ 102
1. Wrexham
2. David Hodgson
3. Marco van Basten
4. Billy Wright
5. Claret and Amber
6. Terry McDermott

QUIZ 103
1. Arbroath
2. Scotland
3. Real Madrid
4. All White
5. Everton
6. Ayr

QUIZ 104
1. Fulham
2. Wales
3. Albania
4. Enzo Scifo
5. Flamengo
6. The Valley (Charlton FC)

QUIZ 105
1. Kilmarnock
2. 'Dixie'
3. Highbury
4. John Charles
5. No.10
6. Sporting Lisbon

QUIZ 106
1. Brian Clough
2. Craig Johnston
3. Rangers
4. 8
5. Eamonn Dunphy
6. The Tango

QUIZ 107
1. Three
2. Hibernian
3. Jan Molby
4. Des Walker
5. Yellow and green
6. Because the referee continually failed to blow for off-sides which the linesman had signalled!

QUIZ 108
1. Ted MacDougall
2. Middlesbrough
3. Dynamo Berlin
4. Colin Clarke
5. Perth
6. The European Cup-Winners Cup

QUIZ 109
1. Brian Clough
2. Chelsea
3. Dynamo Kiev
4. Italy
5. G'ole
6. Tulsa Roughnecks

QUIZ 110
1. Derby County and Nottingham Forest
2. Watford

3. Gloves
4. Athletic Bilbao
5. 'The Judge' (Because they are always on the bench!)
6. West Bromwich Albion

QUIZ 111
1. Rotherham
2. Aberdeen
3. Rob Rensenbrink
4. Gary Lineker
5. He felt that the name 'Pensioners' was inappropriate for his lively young team
6. Stafford

QUIZ 112
1. Denis Law
2. Australia
3. Denmark
4. Zico
5. West Ham
6. Estudiantes

QUIZ 113
1. Trevor Francis
2. Frank, Allan, Derek and Kelvin
3. Plymouth – UEFA ordered them to play 300km from Manchester because of first-leg crowd trouble
4. England
5. Derby County
6. Nobby Stiles

QUIZ 114
1. Hamburg
2. Charlton
3. Bayern Munich
4. Terry Butcher and Graeme Souness
5. George Best
6. Reading and Oxford United

QUIZ 115
1. Rangers
2. Norman Hunter
3. Genoa
4. Green, red and yellow
5. He played in all four divisions in the same season
6. The position of Scottish team manager

QUIZ 116
1. Celtic
2. Andy Townsend
3. Valencia, in 1980
4. Jan Tomaszewski

5. Blue and white hooped jerseys, white shorts and socks
6. The Coronation Cup

QUIZ 117
1. Liverpool
2. Notts County
3. Olympiakos
4. Gerry Francis
5. Luton Town
6. Liverpool

QUIZ 118
1. John Barnwell
2. Emlyn Hughes
3. None – it was played behind closed doors as a result of a disciplinary action by UEFA
4. Windsor Park, Belfast
5. Steve Foster
6. Sunderland

QUIZ 119
1. 5-5
2. Kevin Keegan
3. Dynamo Tbilisi
4. Wales
5. Goodison Park, Everton FC
6. Arthur Ellis

QUIZ 120
1. West Ham
2. Kenny Burns
3. Allan Simonsen
4. Danny McGrain
5. Hull City
6. Players could only be off-side within a line drawn 35 yards from their opponents' goal

QUIZ 121
1. 1965
2. Colin Bell
3. The match was played in their own stadium
4. Liechtenstein
5. Kilmarnock
6. Steve Coppell, at Crystal Palace

QUIZ 122
1. Accrington Stanley
2. John Lukic
3. Arconada
4. Yes, six times
5. Pittodrie, Aberdeen
6. Clyde

QUIZ 123
1. Twelve
2. Leicester City
3. Dropsy
4. West Germany
5. Dark Blue
6. No

QUIZ 124
1. Notts County
2. Larry Lloyd (Liverpool and Forest respectively)
3. Gothenburg, Sweden
4. Peter Taylor
5. Mark Hughes
6. The Azteca

QUIZ 125
1. Queen's Park
2. Leeds United
3. Johnny Metgod
4. Roger Hunt
5. Steve Sherwood
6. West Ham

QUIZ 126
1. Preston North End
2. Aberdeen
3. Porto
4. Mal Donaghy
5. Hitachi
6. An indirect free-kick against the penalty taker for playing the ball twice

QUIZ 127
1. The 1950s
2. Kevin MacDonald
3. University College Dublin
4. Alan Ball
5. 'The Cat'
6. Jock Stein, David Hay, Billy McNeill

QUIZ 128
1. 1958
2. Nicky Walker
3. Old Trafford
4. Ray Clemence
5. Umbro
6. Corner-kick

QUIZ 129
1. Manchester United
2. Derek Dooley
3. George Graham's
4. Carlos Alberto

5. Sky and navy blue
6. Aston Villa, Everton, Dundee United and Rangers

QUIZ 130
1. Division Four
2. Northern Ireland
3. John Bosman
4. Bryan Robson
5. Swansea
6. Mark Hughes

QUIZ 131
1. Tottenham Hotspur
2. Manchester City
3. Stanley Matthews
4. Johan Cruyff
5. The North Bank
6. Stanley Matthews

QUIZ 132
1. Nine
2. Bournemouth
3. Atletico Madrid
4. Don Howe
5. He is a qualified dentist
6. West Bromwich Albion

QUIZ 133
1. Bob Paisley
2. Rangers
3. Sporting Lisbon
4. Scotland
5. Milton Keynes
6. The FA Cup in 1974

QUIZ 134
1. Bradford
2. Phil Neal
3. Hampden Park
4. John Robertson
5. Exeter City
6. Brechin City

QUIZ 135
1. Dave Sexton
2. Coventry City
3. Udo Lattek
4. Alan Ball
5. Black and white striped shirts, black shorts, black socks with white tops
6. Coventry City

QUIZ 136
1. Sharp and Gray
2. Ossie Ardiles

3. The European Cup Winners and the holders of the Cup-Winners Cup
4. Ally MacLeod
5. Fulham's (Craven Cottage)
6. Aston Villa, Chelsea, Man. Utd, Portsmouth, Crystal Palace

QUIZ 137
1. A player-manager
2. Nottingham Forest
3. Swansea City
4. Green
5. 59 minutes 22 seconds
6. Newcastle

QUIZ 138
1. Everton
2. Celtic
3. The Soviet Union
4. Green
5. Brian Clough
6. Bert Millichip

QUIZ 139
1. Sheffield Wednesday
2. Dundee United
3. Birmingham City
4. Pat Rice and Sammy Nelson
5. Queen's Park Rangers, 12 in all
6. A 'Wednesdayite'

QUIZ 140
1. Accrington Stanley
2. Alan McDonald
3. Madeira
4. Alan Rough
5. A Basque
6. Les Cocker

QUIZ 141
1. 'Push and Run'
2. Manchester United
3. Spain
4. 9-3
5. Stoke City
6. London

QUIZ 142
1. Greenhoff
2. Aston Villa
3. Dynamo Zagreb
4. Karl-Heinz Rummenigge
5. Leyton Orient
6. It was the first-ever Football League match to be played on a Sunday

QUIZ 143
1. Northampton Town, from 1960 to 1965
2. Aberdeen
3. Denmark
4. 1971
5. Jimmy Greaves
6. Arsenal

QUIZ 144
1. Liverpool
2. Murdo MacLeod
3. Hungary (Budapest)
4. Trevor Cherry
5. 'Football Crazy'
6. Newcastle

QUIZ 145
1. Tottenham
2. Scunthorpe United
3. Arsenal
4. Hugo Sanchez
5. Carlisle United
6. The Central League

QUIZ 146
1. Crystal Palace
2. Scotland
3. Frankfurt
4. The Soviet Union
5. Sky blue and white striped jerseys, navy shorts and sky blue socks
6. Not necessarily – it may either kick off or take choice of ends

QUIZ 147
1. Jock Wallace
2. Wales
3. Denis Law, in 1964
4. Northern Ireland
5. Burnden Park, Bolton
6. Seville

QUIZ 148
1. Player-manager Kenny Dalglish
2. Fulham
3. Barcelona
4. Dr Joao Havelange
5. The players used them to keep the scores of their card games
6. Jim Platt

QUIZ 149
1. Jimmy Frizzell
2. Clive Allen
3. Wolves
4. Gary Lineker

5. Dundee United
6. Promotion and relegation play-offs

QUIZ 150

1. The introduction of three-points-for-a-win
2. Arsenal
3. Borussia Moenchengladbach
4. Scotland
5. Oldham
6. It occurred in mid-season, rendering all their previous matches void

QUIZ 151

1. Goal difference replaced goal average
2. Bobby Moore
3. Paris
4. Brazil
5. White
6. The winners of the League Cup were to qualify automatically for Europe provided they were a First Division side

QUIZ 152

1. Cambridge United (31 win-less games during 1983-84!)
2. Sunderland
3. Green
4. Jose Luis Brown
5. Morton
6. The Isthmian League

QUIZ 153

1. Arsenal
2. Eire
3. Kevin Keegan
4. Sansom and Rix
5. Tommy Docherty
6. Mike Flanagan

QUIZ 154

1. Swansea City
2. Terry Butcher
3. Athens
4. Liverpool
5. White shirts, black shorts
6. Peru

QUIZ 155

1. Wimbledon
2. Barry Venison
3. Martin Chivers
4. Paul Breitner
5. Jimmy Hill

6. Gordon Taylor

QUIZ 156

1. Ipswich Town
2. Dean Saunders
3. All four clubs came from West Germany
4. Brazil
5. Goal-nets
6. He has been officially cautioned and his name noted

QUIZ 157

1. Reading
2. Billy Thomson
3. AZ 67 Alkmaar
4. Uruguay
5. Blue and white
6. Billy Bingham

QUIZ 158

1. Nottingham Forest
2. Canada
3. Liverpool
4. Northern Ireland and Eire
5. Harry Dowd
6. Seventeen

QUIZ 159

1. Workington
2. Manchester United
3. Bucharest
4. Allan Clarke
5. Bristol Rovers
6. Flamengo

QUIZ 160

1. Bradford Park Avenue
2. Newcastle
3. Hamburg
4. Ernie Brandts
5. Bury
6. The Third Division (North) and Third Division (South) were reformed into Divisions Three and Four

QUIZ 161

1. Arsenal
2. Ray Wilkins
3. Wolves
4. Chris Woods
5. Everton
6. Sheffield United

QUIZ 162

1. Barrow
2. Neil Webb

3. Jurgen Klinsmann
4. Peru
5. Real Madrid
6. Cricket – a bowler taking three successive wickets used to get a new hat

QUIZ 163

1. Gateshead
2. Eire
3. Valencia
4. Holland
5. 'The Hammers'
6. Moscow Dynamo

QUIZ 164

1. Southport
2. Liverpool
3. Nottingham Forest
4. Geoff Hurst, Martin Peters
5. Terry Venables, during his reign in Spain
6. The Southern League

QUIZ 165

1. Preston North End
2. Davie Provan
3. George Best
4. France
5. Falkirk
6. Steve Perryman

QUIZ 166

1. Manchester City
2. Middlesbrough
3. Prague
4. Sky Blue
5. Martin Tyler
6. 1 lb

QUIZ 167

1. Chelsea
2. Gary Mabbutt
3. Tony Parks
4. Brazil's
5. Nottingham Forest
6. Blackburn, Bristol, Doncaster and Tranmere

QUIZ 168

1. 5-1
2. Paul McGrath
3. Bertie Vogts
4. Danny Wallace
5. 22 stone
6. Paris St Germain

QUIZ 169

1. John Sillett and George Curtis
2. Frank McAvennie

3. Manchester United beat Dundee United 5-4 on aggregate
4. Spain
5. Fulham
6. Gemmill, McGovern and O'Hare

QUIZ 170

1. Ron Saunders
2. Coventry City
3. Benfica
4. John Barnes
5. Danny Blanchflower
6. They were father and son

QUIZ 171

1. Harry Catterick
2. Remi Moses
3. Iain Ferguson
4. Guadalajara
5. Brown
6. Billy Bremner and Kevin Keegan

QUIZ 172

1. Bertie Mee
2. Oxford United
3. All white
4. Peter Shilton
5. Albion Rovers
6. Watford

QUIZ 173

1. Sunderland
2. Pat Nevin
3. SV Hamburg
4. A red diagonal band
5. He helped mounted policeman George Scorey clear the pitch after an overspill of spectators
6. 200,000

QUIZ 174

1. Aberdeen
2. Birmingham City
3. Jorge Valdano
4. Northern Ireland (Because of the political situation)
5. By throwing ticker-tape
6. The Divisions Three and Four clubs

QUIZ 175

1. Manchester City
2. Norwegian
3. Anderlecht
4. Gary Sprake
5. Cliftonville
6. Wolves

QUIZ 176
1. Leeds United
2. Colchester United
3. Graeme Souness
4. Willie Miller
5. Plymouth Argyle
6. South America (It's their equivalent of the European Cup)

QUIZ 177
1. Leeds United
2. Wales
3. Everton, the Cup-Winners Cup in 1985
4. Manchester United
5. Blue
6. Bury

QUIZ 178
1. Middlesbrough
2. Wales
3. QPR in 1984
4. The USA
5. 29 times
6. Stan Flashman

QUIZ 179
1. The Football League Second Division Championship
2. Jimmy Nicholl
3. Dundee United
4. Six
5. A defeat in which the losing team did not walk off in anger before the final whistle!
6. Huddersfield

QUIZ 180
1. Joe Fagan
2. Manchester City
3. Stan Bowles
4. Steve Coppell
5. Red and yellow
6. 114

QUIZ 181
1. It became the first club to automatically lose its League status as a result of finishing bottom of Division Four
2. The Republic of Ireland
3. Nine
4. Scotland
5. Villa Park
6. Charlie Nicholas

QUIZ 182
1. Millwall
2. Liverpool
3. West Germany
4. Northern Ireland
5. Tottenham Hotspur's
6. Millwall

QUIZ 183
1. Matt Busby
2. Elton John
3. Karl-Heinz Rummenigge
4. He was the linesman who signalled that Geoff Hurst's shot had crossed the line to put England 3-2 up in the World Cup Final
5. Brighton
6. Tokyo

QUIZ 184
1. Liverpool
2. Kevin Reeves
3. Rangers
4. Scotland 0 England 5
5. Portsmouth
6. Lou Macari

QUIZ 185
1. Queen's Park Rangers
2. Norwich
3. Derby County
4. John Wark
5. Fulham
6. John Wark

QUIZ 186
1. Every one was an all-London affair
2. The USA
3. Leeds, Liverpool, Tottenham
4. Derek Spence
5. Airdrie
6. Chelsea, Leeds, Ipswich and Manchester City

QUIZ 187
1. Terry Butcher
2. Manchester City
3. Ajax Amsterdam
4. Zico
5. Amber and Black
6. John Barnwell

QUIZ 188
1. Tottenham
2. Phil Parkes
3. Glasgow

4. Gordon Cowans
5. ... Parrot'
6. The Golden Boot

QUIZ 189
1. Nottingham Forest in 1978, Arsenal in 1987
2. Coventry City
3. Aberdeen
4. Mike Smith
5. Tony Galvin
6. No, it must be at least 5 feet high

QUIZ 190
1. Aston Villa
2. Manchester City
3. Valencia
4. Paraguay
5. Brian Glanville
6. Brian Horton

QUIZ 191
1. Liverpool
2. Ipswich Town
3. 6-0 to Liverpool
4. Light blue and white striped jersey with black shorts and white socks
5. Leighton James
6. Manchester United

QUIZ 192
1. Tottenham
2. Tony Morley
3. Paolo Rossi
4. Blue
5. Bobby Robson
6. Wolves

QUIZ 193
1. Aston Villa
2. Mick Channon
3. West Germany
4. Bruce Rioch
5. Yellow shirts with red and black trim, black shorts and red socks
6. Joe Jordan and Gordon McQueen

QUIZ 194
1. Stoke City
2. A loss (of approximately £400,000)
3. Monaco
4. Johan Cruyff
5. Ibrox Stadium
6. Three-up and three-down replaced two-up and two-down

QUIZ 195
1. Everton
2. Southampton

3. Norway
4. Daniel Passarella
5. *Gregory's Girl*
6. 15

QUIZ 196
1. Ronnie Whelan
2. Manchester United
3. Boniek
4. Alan Giresse
5. Grimsby Town
6. Tottenham Hotspur

QUIZ 197
1. The FA Cup
2. Tom Finney
3. Benfica
4. Cameroon
5. *Onze*
6. Nine

QUIZ 198
1. Chris Woods
2. Bolton
3. Feyenoord
4. Hungary
5. The title was awarded to Scotland's World Cup squad
6. Andy Ritchie

QUIZ 199
1. Wolves
2. Kevin Richardson
3. Inter-Milan
4. Leicester City
5. Manchester City
6. Telford United

QUIZ 200
1. Aston Villa
2. Partick Thistle
3. Yellow
4. Peru
5. Arsenal
6. They are two separate Leagues. The Irish League is for Northern Ireland's clubs, the League of Ireland being contested in the Republic

QUIZ 201
1. Emlyn Hughes
2. Chester
3. Dark Blue
4. Joe Jordan
5. Peterborough
6. It was a header

QUIZ 202
1. Maurice Evans
2. Orient
3. Red and White stripes
4. Rivelino
5. Hudson's shot had hit the stanchion outside the goal and rebounded into play. However, the referee thought it had entered the net and so awarded a goal
6. Port Vale

QUIZ 203
1. Swindon Town
2. Tommy Smith
3. Alan Sealey
4. Austria
5. Rangers
6. South American (17 times to 10)

QUIZ 204
1. Clive Walker
2. Liverpool
3. Boavista
4. Belgium
5. 'The Group of Sleep'
6. August

QUIZ 205
1. Nottingham Forest
2. Paul Cooper
3. Red and White
4. Peru
5. Plymouth Argyle, Exeter City and Torquay United
6. Tommy Docherty

QUIZ 206
1. Asa Hartford
2. Manchester United
3. Juventus
4. Rene Van der Kerkhof
5. Ken Bates
6. They were banned for one season following a pitched battle between their fans and the Barcelona police

QUIZ 207
1. John Toshack
2. Graeme Sharp
3. White and Blue
4. Kuwait
5. Jimmy Hill
6. Frank Clark

QUIZ 208
1. Graeme Souness
2. Paul Gascoigne
3. Brian Kidd
4. Australia
5. 'Bald Eagle'
6. Sheffield Wednesday

QUIZ 209
1. Bobby Moore
2. Leeds
3. Red and black
4. Peru
5. Ninian Park
6. Kenny Burns

QUIZ 210
1. Chris Woods (Rangers)
2. Nigel Spink
3. Sky blue
4. 1974
5. Bobby Moore
6. Barclays

QUIZ 211
1. Five
2. Leicester City
3. Aberdeen
4. Goalkeeper Gordon Banks
5. AFC Bournemouth
6. The UEFA Cup

QUIZ 212
1. Steve Perryman
2. Adrian Heath
3. Liverpool
4. Argentina
5. Everton
6. A penalty-kick

QUIZ 213
1. Charlie Nicholas
2. Kevin
3. Blue and red stripes
4. Boniek
5. Lawrie McMenemy
6. Racing Club

QUIZ 214
1. Manchester United
2. Didier Six
3. Juventus
4. Carlos Manuel
5. Dundee and Dundee United
6. They played off for third place

QUIZ 215
1. Leicester City
2. Jamaica
3. All white with a thick red vertical centre-panel down front and back

4. Uruguay
5. George Best
6. Leicester City and Brentford

QUIZ 216

1. Bolton
2. Paul Sturrock
3. Steaua Bucharest
4. West Ham
5. Don McVicar!
6. 130 Yards

QUIZ 217

1. Hereford United
2. Hibernian and Celtic
3. Sky Blue
4. Swiss
5. Sam Leitch
6. New York Cosmos

QUIZ 218

1. Billy Bonds
2. 6ft 4ins
3. Grasshoppers
4. Archie Gemmill
5. Terry Venables
6. None

QUIZ 219

1. Score in an FA Cup Final
2. Gordon Strachan
3. Monaco
4. Cabrini
5. Linfield
6. Lou Macari (Swindon Town)

QUIZ 220

1. Frank Lampard
2. Chelsea
3. Panathinaikos
4. 'The Group of Death'
5. A submarine
6. Three

QUIZ 221

1. Jackie Milburn
2. Davie Cooper
3. 1968
4. Luther Blissett
5. Rod Stewart
6. Wolves

QUIZ 222

1. Tottenham Hotspur in 1901 (They were then still in the Southern League)
2. Kenny Swain

3. A red star!
4. Chile
5. Dixie Dean
6. The European Nations Championship

QUIZ 223

1. Stan Mortensen
2. Peter Marinello
3. Royal
4. Gerd Muller
5. Clyde, Partick Thistle, Queen's Park
6. Rangers

QUIZ 224

1. Bolton
2. Hearts
3. Holland
4. Cesar Luis Menotti
5. 5ft 1in
6. Both sides keep the trophy for six months each

QUIZ 225

1. Liverpool
2. West Ham
3. Alexander Zavarov
4. Sweden
5. Arsenal
6. Manchester United in 1958 – as a gesture by UEFA following the Munich air crash

QUIZ 226

1. Cardiff City
2. Southampton
3. Anderlecht
4. Scotland
5. Crystal Palace
6. The Football League Cup

QUIZ 227

1. Bert Trautmann
2. Liverpool
3. Austria
4. Graeme Souness
5. A horse
6. The Watney Cup

QUIZ 228

1. *Alan* Sunderland scored the winner – for Arsenal!
2. Brighton
3. AC Milan
4. All red
5. He had already been capped – for Eire!

6. Swansea City

QUIZ 229
1. John Duncan
2. Ray Stewart
3. The Volksparkstadion
4. 'Total Football'
5. Gerald Sinstadt
6. The Football Combination

QUIZ 230
1. West Bromwich Albion
2. Burnley
3. The Nep stadium, Budapest
4. Clive Thomas
5. 'Aztec Lightning'
6. Test Matches

QUIZ 231
1. Everton
2. QPR
3. John Robertson
4. Blackpool
5. Albert Camus
6. Only one club per city was allowed to enter

QUIZ 232
1. Leeds United
2. Gordon Banks
3. Benfica
4. Dino Zoff
5. Heart of Midlothian
6. Andy Gray

QUIZ 233
1. Mick Jones
2. Jimmy Case
3. Rumania
4. Being their third victory, they were allowed to keep the trophy
5. Frank Bough
6. Scotland – he was Secretary of the SFA

QUIZ 234
1. Manchester City
2. Trevor Senior
3. Feyenoord
4. Chelsea
5. Blue
6. South America's equivalent of UEFA

QUIZ 235
1. Ian St John (for Liverpool against Leeds)
2. Ian Stewart
3. Valencia

4. Wales
5. Paul Reaney
6. Almost eight years

QUIZ 236
1. Allan Clarke
2. Gary Lineker
3. Switzerland (Berne)
4. Bossis
5. Liverpool
6. The Rest of the World

QUIZ 237
1. Geoff Barnett
2. Ajax
3. Michel Platini
4. 'El Loco'
5. Queen's Park
6. The second round

QUIZ 238
1. Eddie Kelly
2. Kevin Moran
3. Lenin Stadium, Moscow (102,000)
4. Viv Anderson
5. Jimmy Hill
6. Sir Alf Ramsey

QUIZ 239
1. Ray Kennedy
2. AC Milan
3. Rangers
4. Lato
5. The League of Ireland
6. Winger

QUIZ 240
1. Charlie George
2. Glynn and Ian
3. St Etienne
4. The German Democratic Republic (East Germany)
5. Crystal Palace
6. The home associations feel that to have an integrated Great Britain side might jeopardise their right to field four separate UK teams in the World Cup

QUIZ 241
1. Rotherham United
2. Dave Thomas
3. Enschede
4. Red
5. Ray Houghton (who plays for Eire)
6. $1\frac{1}{2}$

QUIZ 242

1. Leicester City
2. Ipswich and Arsenal
3. Lazio
4. Jim Holton
5. Blue and white
6. He was the Football League Secretary

QUIZ 243

1. Peter Shilton
2. Danny Thomas
3. Paris St Germain and Racing Club de Paris
4. 54
5. Two, Cardiff and Swansea
6. A 'Nutmeg'

QUIZ 244

1. Wimbledon
2. No.5
3. Borussia Moenchengladbach
4. Norman Whiteside
5. Selhurst Park
6. Wimbledon

QUIZ 245

1. Hearts
2. Kenny Clements
3. Dalymount Park
4. Turkey
5. 'Butch'
6. Maine Road (Old Trafford had suffered bomb damage during the war)

QUIZ 246

1. Fulham
2. Peter Beardsley
3. FK Austria
4. Paolo Rossi
5. He was scared of flying
6. Manchester United

QUIZ 247

1. Alan Taylor
2. Cologne
3. Anderlecht
4. Italy
5. John Lloyd
6. Brazil

QUIZ 248

1. Kevin Keegan
2. Norwich
3. Juventus
4. 'The Hand of God'
5. Terry Venables
6. Derby County

QUIZ 249

1. Ian Porterfield
2. Paul Walsh
3. Bayern Munich
4. Jim Leighton
5. West Bromwich Albion
6. Lilleshall

QUIZ 250

1. Jim Montgomery
2. Paul Ince
3. Igor Belanov
4. Mark Hateley
5. 'Scotsport'
6. Athletic Bilbao

QUIZ 251

1. Malcom Macdonald
2. Ray Wilkins
3. Olympiakos
4. Italy
5. Pickles
6. Exeter, Halifax, Oxford, Wrexham, Crewe Alexandra

QUIZ 252

1. Stuart Pearson
2. Morgan
3. Manchester City
4. Poland
5. Kevin Keegan
6. Charlton, Oldham, Wigan

QUIZ 253

1. Peter Rodrigues
2. Alex Young
3. Juventus
4. Willie Johnston
5. Bryan Robson
6. Billy Bremner

QUIZ 254

1. Ron Greenwood
2. Mark Walters
3. Benfica
4. Jimmy Greaves
5. Old Gold
6. They were broken by celebrating Scots fans

QUIZ 255

1. Jim McCalliog
2. John Wark
3. Real Madrid

4. Pumpido
5. Alf Ramsey
6. He was the first substitute used in a Football League match

QUIZ 256
1. Peter Osgood
2. Viv Anderson
3. Red Star Belgrade
4. The holders
5. They considered them to be too brutal!
6. Manchester United

QUIZ 257
1. Brian Talbot
2. Jim Bett
3. Rotterdam
4. David Narey
5. Harold Wilson
6. Rangers

QUIZ 258
1. Jimmy Greenhoff
2. Scotland
3. Alan Kennedy
4. Mexico
5. Motherwell
6. Goal Average – used in the League prior to 1976

QUIZ 259
1. Motherwell
2. Southampton
3. Bruges
4. Jules Rimet
5. He continually beats a drum
6. No

QUIZ 260
1. Arsenal
2. John White
3. Moscow
4. Andy Roxburgh
5. It was named after the Spion Kop, a hill defended by British troops during the Boer War
6. Dave Bassett

QUIZ 261
1. Roger Osborne
2. Nigeria
3. Liege
4. Wales
5. 'This Time'
6. It was played on a home-and-away basis

QUIZ 262
1. Mick Mills of Stoke City
2. Norman Whiteside
3. Belgium
4. Uruguay
5. Sheffield United
6. Eight

QUIZ 263
1. Huddersfield Town
2. Peter Fox
3. CSKA Sofia
4. 1958
5. They were originally called Southampton St Mary's
6. Wolverhampton Wanderers

QUIZ 264
1. Tony Cascarino
2. Ron Harris
3. Cologne
4. Uruguay
5. Carlisle United
6. Terry Venables

QUIZ 265
1. The sixth round (quarter-finals)
2. Ally MacLeod
3. Mark Lawrenson
4. Joe Corrigan
5. A cannon
6. A corner-kick

QUIZ 266
1. One (Mark Lawrenson, who was born in Preston)
2. Paul and Ron Futcher
3. Czechoslovakia
4. Scotland
5. Yellow (it used to be reserved for internationals only)
6. The third round

QUIZ 267
1. Preston North End
2. Graeme Sharp
3. Jupp Heynckes
4. France
5. Hibernian
6. England, by 6 - 4

QUIZ 268
1. Chelsea
2. Peter Latchford
3. Denmark
4. Holland
5. Scunthorpe

6. John Toshack

QUIZ 269
1. Frank Stapleton
2. Ipswich Town
3. Dynamo Kiev
4. North Korea
5. Granada
6. Millwall

QUIZ 270
1. Liverpool
2. Manchester City
3. Corsica
4. Steve Coppell's
5. Sheffield
6. Blackburn

QUIZ 271
1. Brian Kidd
2. Wales
3. Carl Zeiss Jena
4. Anfield, Liverpool
5. Maroon
6. Rio de Janeiro

QUIZ 272
1. Wolverhampton Wanderers
2. Jackie Milburn
3. Olympiakos
4. Jock Stein
5. Hibs
6. Phil Neal

QUIZ 273
1. West Ham, in 1980
2. Trevor Francis
3. Cardiff
4. West Germany
5. The Stretford End
6. Northern Ireland

QUIZ 274
1. Trevor Brooking
2. Stewart Houston
3. Michel Platini
4. Socrates
5. A tree
6. Alan Hardaker

QUIZ 275
1. Hibernian
2. Willie Johnston
3. Iceland
4. Ferenc Puskas
5. Terry Ramsden
6. Australia

QUIZ 276
1. Manchester City
2. Jim Duffy
3. Fiorentina
4. Billy Hamilton
5. Yellow
6. Arsenal and Huddersfield

QUIZ 277
1. Because of the Falklands confict with Argentina, it was considered politically insensitive to play him
2. Goalkeeper Alex Stepney (with 2 penalties)
3. Peter Osgood
4. Sky blue shirts, black shorts
5. York City
6. Tampa Bay Rowdies

QUIZ 278
1. Graham Roberts
2. Frank Gray (for Leeds and Nottingham Forest)
3. Luxembourg
4. Orange
5. Berwick Rangers
6. The Charity Shield match

QUIZ 279
1. Southport
2. Mark Hughes
3. Malta
4. Uruguay
5. John Sillett
6. Hugo

QUIZ 280
1. Queen's Park Rangers
2. Chelsea, Stoke and Arsenal
3. Juventus
4. Willie Ormond
5. Aberdeen and Wimbledon
6. The FA Trophy

QUIZ 281
1. Celtic
2. Don Rogers
3. Alkmaar
4. Queen's Park
5. *Goal*
6. Seattle

QUIZ 282
1. West Bromwich Albion
2. Wales
3. Manchester United
4. Luis Pereira

5. Graeme Souness'
6. Denis Law

QUIZ 283
1. Garth Crooks
2. AC Milan
3. Go Ahead
4. There wasn't a final in that year's competition – only a final pool played on a league basis and won by Uruguay!
5. Cricket
6. They held a ballot among their fans!

QUIZ 284
1. Manchester United
2. Andy King
3. Steve Perryman
4. Blue
5. *Shoot*
6. Spurs

QUIZ 285
1. Jimmy Melia
2. Peter Knowles
3. Norway
4. Mo Johnston
5. Penny
6. They were sent off

QUIZ 286
1. They have each been top First Division goalscorer for a particular season
2. Sheffield United
3. IFK Gothenburg
4. Enzo Bearzot
5. Billy Wright
6. United

QUIZ 287
1. Arsenal
2. 'Pop'
3. Berne
4. Eusebio
5. Blue, white and red
6. Zico

QUIZ 288
1. Gordon Smith
2. Stanley Matthews
3. Poland
4. Jimmy Johnstone
5. Subbuteo
6. A player taking the throw from the wrong place is now penalized by the throw being awarded to the opposition

QUIZ 289
1. Burnley
2. Sunderland
3. Lodz
4. France
5. The Hawthorns
6. 80

QUIZ 290
1. Gary Stevens
2. Joey Jones
3. Sporting Lisbon
4. 25
5. Hibernian
6. Tony Cottee

QUIZ 291
1. Stoke City
2. Burnley, Everton, Chelsea, Notts County, Brentford and Arsenal
3. Benfica
4. 1983, against Uruguay at Hampden
5. Rangers
6. Twelve

QUIZ 292
1. Watford
2. Steve Archibald
3. Yugoslavia
4. Billy Wright
5. 'The Vulture'
6. He has already played in the competition for another team and so is ineligible to appear for his present club

QUIZ 293
1. Plymouth Argyle, in 1984
2. West Ham
3. No.14
4. Tarantini
5. Brazil and Jordan
6. The toss of a coin

QUIZ 294
1. Brighton
2. Millwall
3. Rumania
4. Davie Cooper
5. Coventry City
6. Five

QUIZ 295
1. Bournemouth
2. Phil Thompson

3. Bangor City
4. He scored in every round including the Final
5. Desmond Morris
6. The Multipart League

QUIZ 296
1. Telford United
2. McAdam
3. Espanol
4. Belgium
5. Manchester United
6. Rochdale (Danny Bergara)

QUIZ 297
1. York
2. Gordon Hill
3. Pamplona
4. Martin O'Neill
5. 'Bamber Gascoigne'
6. Yes, seven times to five

QUIZ 298
1. Ron Atkinson
2. Eire
3. Real Mallorca
4. Lato
5. Peter Reid
6. Dundee United

QUIZ 299
1. Kevin Moran
2. Billy McNeill
3. Cardiff and Derry City
4. The Soviet Union
5. Richard Gough
6. Billy McNeill

QUIZ 300
1. Norman Whiteside
2. Derby County
3. San Sebastian
4. Jack Taylor
5. A bible
6. Kenny Dalglish

QUIZ 301
1. Manchester City's
2. Ian Wallace
3. Sweden
4. Franz Beckenbauer
5. White and red
6. 'Playing advantage'

QUIZ 302
1. Celtic
2. Glenn Roeder

3. Ray Crawford
4. Czechoslovakia
5. Argentina
6. The kick-off and penalty-kick

QUIZ 303
1. Mo Johnston
2. Norwich City
3. Eusebio
4. It was a four-way tie
5. Clive Walker
6. The paddock

QUIZ 304
1. They all played for Leeds
2. Morton, AC Milan, Verona
3. Young Boys (Berne)
4. Scotland
5. The City Ground, Nottingham
6. Derek Johnstone

QUIZ 305
1. Mark Wright
2. Martin Peters
3. Udinese
4. Wales
5. A fight which broke out between rival camera crews!
6. No

QUIZ 306
1. Everton
2. Paddy Roche
3. Switzerland
4. Poland
5. Derry City
6. Five

QUIZ 307
1. Liverpool, in the FA Cup Final
2. Wallace
3. Zurich
4. George Best
5. Leyton Orient
6. Allan Clarke

QUIZ 308
1. Ian Rush
2. Manchester United
3. Istanbul
4. Norway
5. Scotland
6. City

QUIZ 309
1. Tottenham and QPR in 1982
2. Tony

3. Renat Dasayev
4. New Zealand
5. Birmingham City
6. Celtic

QUIZ 310

1. Manchester United's Kevin Moran, who had been sent off. The FA later decided to award him his medal
2. Steve Nicol
3. Denis Law
4. Garrincha
5. He flicked the ball up with both heels, donkey-style, for team-mate Ernie Hunt to volley a famous goal
6. Howard Kendall

QUIZ 311

1. Yes
2. Mickey Walsh
3. Dynamo Kiev
4. Denmark
5. 4 seconds
6. He played for Wales

QUIZ 312

1. Gary Gillespie
2. David Speedie
3. Leningrad
4. Bobby Moore
5. Stanley Matthews
6. Yes, the referee should award an indirect free-kick against the player for ungentlemanly conduct

QUIZ 313

1. Scarborough
2. Nottingham Forest's
3. The European Super Cup match between the European Cup winners and the holders of the Cup Winners Cup
4. Mexico
5. Huddersfield Town
6. Canon

QUIZ 314

1. Wigan
2. Andy Lochead
3. Juventus
4. Leeds United (Lorimer and Jordan)
5. White shirts, navy shorts and white socks
6. They were played on a two-leg basis

QUIZ 315

1. Nottingham Forest
2. Graeme Souness
3. Bavaria, a region of Germany
4. Patrick Battiston
5. Chelsea
6. Holland and Belgium

QUIZ 316

1. Chelsea
2. Belgium
3. It is the year of formation – 1904
4. Twice, 1978 and 1986
5. Leicester
6. Willie Ormond

QUIZ 317

1. Bruce Grobbelaar
2. Sheffield United
3. Graham Rix
4. Luis Fernandez
5. They failed to pay their annual dues!
6. Newcastle (he's better known as Mirandinha)

QUIZ 318

1. Chris Woods
2. Chelsea
3. AC Milan
4. Red and white stripes
5. Notts County
6. The World Club Championship

QUIZ 319

1. Rangers
2. John Toshack
3. It is the name of a national hero
4. Trevor Francis
5. Wembley
6. In the early days, a player was off-side unless THREE opponents (compared to TWO nowadays) were between him and the goal

QUIZ 320

1. Rangers
2. Mickey Thomas
3. Internazionale
4. Bulgaria
5. Liverpool
6. Players' names

QUIZ 321

1. Edinburgh rivals Hibs
2. Ronnie Whelan
3. Vitkovice
4. Helmut Schoen

5. Dundee United
6. Burnley

QUIZ 322
1. Celtic
2. Norman Whiteside
3. Malta
4. Marco Tardelli
5. Cambridge United
6. They all played in the capital Montevideo

QUIZ 323
1. Dumbarton
2. Geoff Hurst
3. Yugoslavia
4. Holland
5. The district of the city in which they play was formerly called Owlerton
6. No

QUIZ 324
1. Celtic
2. QPR
3. They are all army teams
4. Howard Kendall
5. Blue and yellow
6. The Football League

QUIZ 325
1. Kilmarnock
2. Ipswich Town
3. Real Madrid
4. The Scottish Premier League
5. Mike Yarwood
6. Yes, Portsmouth who won it in 1939 and 'held' it until the next competition in 1946

QUIZ 326
1. Jock Stein
2. Manchester United
3. Valencia
4. Dave Mitchell, who played for Australia
5. St Andrews (Birmingham City)
6. 8 yards

QUIZ 327
1. Derby County
2. England
3. Mickey Walsh (Porto)
4. Mazzola
5. Queen's Park Rangers
6. Northern Ireland

QUIZ 328
1. Nottingham Forest and Norwich
2. Newcastle
3. Berlin
4. Joe Jordan of Scotland (The referee believed that it was a Welsh arm which played the ball)
5. They wanted to play a record of England's Wembley crowd cheering
6. Birmingham

QUIZ 329
1. The 'Lisbon Lions'
2. Billy Wright
3. East Germany
4. Brazil
5. Paul Allen
6. The referee should penalize the player only if he considers that a opponent was distracted by the shout

QUIZ 330
1. Alex MacDonald
2. Peter Houseman
3. Italy's
4. Goodison Park
5. Red and white
6. Uruguay

QUIZ 331
1. Alex Ferguson
2. Newport County
3. Rapid Vienna
4. Greece
5. Blue and white
6. Franz Beckenbauer (Bayern Munich and West Germany)

QUIZ 332
1. Preston North End, in 1964
2. Asa Hartford
3. Juventus and Torino
4. He submitted a positive dope test
5. Portsmouth
6. Jimmy Greaves'

QUIZ 333
1. Hearts
2. Wolves
3. Czechoslovakia
4. Thirteen
5. Sean Connery
6. He has managed two World Cup-winning sides (Italy, 1934 and 1938)

QUIZ 334
1. No
2. Notts County
3. Yugoslavia
4. Spain
5. Shamrock Rovers
6. Arsenal

QUIZ 335
1. Celtic
2. Wales
3. Horst Hrubesch
4. Alex Ferguson
5. Blue and gold
6. A goal-kick

QUIZ 336
1. It clinched the 1986-87 championship for Everton
2. Dennis Tueart
3. Marco Tardelli's
4. Chile
5. Pittodrie Stadium, Aberdeen
6. Liverpool

QUIZ 337
1. Walter Kidd
2. Alan Kennedy and Terry McDermott
3. Denmark
4. George Courtney
5. Julian Wilson
6. England team manager

QUIZ 338
1. He had left to join the Argentina squad in preparation for the 1982 World Cup
2. He was the first £1000 player
3. Johan Cruyff
4. Uruguay
5. Loftus Road
6. Scored for both teams

QUIZ 339
1. Hibernian
2. Frank Stapleton
3. Yugoslavia
4. Colombia
5. 'Life at the Kop'
6. Chile

QUIZ 340
1. Queen's Park
2. Steve Heighway
3. Belgium
4. They have each won only one cap

5. Because going out onto the pitch first would have upset his superstitious pre-match routines
6. Sao Paulo

QUIZ 341
1. Jock Wallace
2. Johnny Haynes
3. Kevin Keegan
4. Neza
5. An electrified fence
6. He was the first £100-a-week footballer

QUIZ 342
1. John Bond
2. Billy Wright
3. Greece
4. Argentina and Italy
5. 'Abide With Me'
6. Yes

QUIZ 343
1. East Fife
2. Bobby Mimms
3. Phil Neal
4. Iran
5. West Bromwich Albion
6. Malta

QUIZ 344
1. Celtic
2. Frank Worthington
3. Italy
4. Yellow shirts and blue shorts
5. The Jules Rimet Trophy (World Cup)
6. The League Champions

QUIZ 345
1. Aberdeen
2. David Johnson
3. The Soviet Union
4. Mario Kempes
5. Millwall
6. It has the lowest-ever official League attendance – 13!

QUIZ 346
1. Preston North End
2. Frank Swift
3. Albania
4. Yes, two
5. 'The Wave'
6. Yes

QUIZ 347
1. West Bromwich Albion
2. Ron Yeats

3. Bayern Munich
4. 1958
5. Giants Stadium, East Rutherford, New Jersey
6. Yes, provided the referee has signalled that he may do so

QUIZ 348
1. 16
2. Viv Anderson
3. The Soviet Union
4. The hosts, Brazil
5. Amber and black
6. His club Southampton were relegated

QUIZ 349
1. George McCluskey
2. Yours truly, Bob Wilson
3. Wales
4. Israel
5. Bradford City
6. Nacional of Uruguay

QUIZ 350
1. Portsmouth
2. Gary Bailey
3. Dieter Muller
4. Zurich
5. Carrow Road, Norwich
6. Martin Hodge

QUIZ 351
1. Danny McGrain
2. John Fashanu
3. Larry Lloyd
4. Yes, Brazil in 1958
5. Vale Park, Port Vale FC
6. Shrewsbury Town

QUIZ 352
1. Eric Black
2. Ray Kennedy
3. Malta
4. The *libero*
5. Graham Roberts'
6. Steve Ogrizovic

QUIZ 353
1. The 1983-84 Final was played in March and the 1984-85 Final took place in October
2. Derby County
3. Spain
4. England, Northern Ireland, Scotland and Denmark
5. Bruce Grobbelaar's
6. St Mirren

QUIZ 354
1. Dens Park, home of neighbours Dundee
2. Ron Radford of Hereford United
3. Crete
4. Northern Ireland
5. Rugby League
6. 6-6

QUIZ 355
1. Terry Fenwick
2. Peter Barnes
3. Gunter Netzer
4. Portugal
5. White
6. For violent conduct towards his own players

QUIZ 356
1. Partick Thistle
2. Alan Biley
3. *Catenaccio*
4. Hungary
5. Manchester
6. Terry Dolan

QUIZ 357
1. Doug Rougvie
2. Mitchell Thomas
3. Yellow and blue
4. Willy and Rene Van der Kerkhof in 1978
5. Sheffield United
6. Argentina

QUIZ 358
1. Gordon Wallace
2. West Bromwich Albion
3. Tony Woodcock and Kevin Keegan
4. Seven
5. Craig Johnston
6. The current holders

QUIZ 359
1. 'Lucky Arsenal'
2. They are both diabetics
3. Sweden
4. Mario Zagalo
5. Sammy Nelson
6. Tony Adams

QUIZ 360
1. Aberdeen
2. Trevor Francis
3. Real Madrid

4. John McClelland, for Northern Ireland
5. Bob Paisley
6. Gary Ablett

QUIZ 361

1. John Hewitt
2. Manchester City
3. Bayern Munich
4. Red
5. Eddie Gray
6. It was the first 'Match of the Day' on BBC Television

QUIZ 362

1. 1984
2. Nottingham Forest
3. New York Cosmos
4. The Soviet Union
5. Luton Town
6. Rotherham

QUIZ 363

1. Dundee
2. Tony Norman
3. Hungary
4. Bobby Charlton
5. Brian Clough
6. He was ordered off

QUIZ 364

1. Archie Gemmill
2. Steve Ogrizovic
3. Real Madrid
4. Red, white and green
5. Swansea and Wrexham
6. He knocked out the referee!

QUIZ 365

1. It is the fastest goal in Scottish Cup history (9.6 seconds)
2. West Bromwich Albion
3. Oleg Blokhin, formerly of Dynamo Kiev
4. Italy
5. 'Bulldog Bobby'
6. Jim Beglin

QUIZ 366

1. 1919
2. Len Shackleton
3. Hungary
4. Jeff Astle
5. Rotherham
6. Ray Clemence

QUIZ 367

1. Phil Boyer
2. Clive Allen

3. Dominique Rocheteau
4. Bulgaria
5. Hearts
6. St Mirren

QUIZ 368

1. Manchester City
2. Peter Bonetti
3. Madrid
4. Rudi Voller
5. Tottenham's
6. No, if they were national champions they would play in the European Cup the following season

QUIZ 369

1. Martin Buchan
2. Gary Mills
3. Barcelona
4. Manager
5. Pat Crerand
6. Hamilton Accies

QUIZ 370

1. Billy Bremner
2. John Charles
3. Rumania
4. Terry Butcher
5. Meadowbank Thistle
6. Denis Howell

QUIZ 371

1. Everton
2. Wales
3. Benfica
4. Australia
5. Jim Herriot
6. English clubs which had qualified for Europe but were unable to compete because of the UEFA ban

QUIZ 372

1. Tony Book
2. Peter Beardsley
3. AS Roma
4. Greece
5. Jimmy Johnstone
6. Burnley

QUIZ 373

1. Wolves
2. Preston
3. Johan Cruyff
4. Terry Butcher
5. The County Ground, Swindon
6. Because he did not want to be tagged 'The First £100,000 Player'

QUIZ 374
1. Derby County
2. George Best
3. Spartak Moscow
4. Tottenham
5. Deepdale, Preston
6. He was in jail for driving offences

QUIZ 375
1. Billy McNeill
2. Blackburn
3. Poland
4. Kenny Dalglish
5. Christian
6. Ian Callaghan of Liverpool

QUIZ 376
1. Stoke City
2. Chelsea
3. East Germany
4. Hungary
5. 'Smash and Grab'
6. The Football Writers' Association

QUIZ 377
1. Leicester City
2. Manchester City
3. Mauve
4. Joe Mercer, on a caretaker basis
5. Kevin Keegan
6. Derek Statham

QUIZ 378
1. Rangers
2. John McClelland
3. Holland
4. Pele
5. Azteca
6. Hereford

QUIZ 379
1. Derek Johnstone
2. Australia
3. Ajax
4. Franz Beckenbauer
5. St James' Park, Newcastle
6. Nantes

QUIZ 380
1. Leeds United
2. Lee Sharpe
3. Roger Davies
4. The USA
5. *Hero*
6. Joe Jordan

QUIZ 381
1. Pat Jennings
2. Sweeper
3. Real Madrid
4. Wales
5. Viv Richards
6. Alex Ferguson

QUIZ 382
1. Watford
2. Trevor Francis, Ian Wallace and Justin Fashanu
3. Hungary
4. 1970, against East Germany
5. Grimsby Town
6. 'Intermediate'

QUIZ 383
1. £10,000
2. Brian Stein
3. They swapped their navy shorts and socks for an all-white kit
4. France
5. Rugby
6. Arsenal

QUIZ 384
1. Don Howe
2. Gordon Smith
3. Gerd Muller
4. Joe Baker
5. Amber and blue
6. He holds his arm aloft until the ball is touched by a second player

QUIZ 385
1. Kevin Keegan
2. Carlisle United
3. Johan Neeskins
4. West Germany
5. Sixth
6. It came from three penalties

QUIZ 386
1. None
2. Atletico Madrid
3. Michel Platini
4. Denis Law's
5. Stamford Bridge, Chelsea
6. Yes, but only if the game has not been restarted

QUIZ 387
1. Bob Latchford
2. Leicester City
3. Austria
4. Scotland, who won 3-2 at Wembley in 1967
5. Reading
6. Because of their refusal to offer tickets to visitors Cardiff City

QUIZ 388
1. Denis Law
2. Aston Villa
3. Hans Krankl
4. Eoin Hand
5. Elland Road, Leeds
6. 10-0 to the home side in both cases

QUIZ 389
1. Manchester United
2. Dave Watson
3. Nottingham Forest
4. Alf Ramsey (32 caps)
5. Arsenal
6. The Women's FA Cup

QUIZ 390
1. Glenn Hoddle
2. Ian Ure
3. Barcelona
4. Noel Brotherston
5. Craig Johnston
6. Cyril Knowles

QUIZ 391
1. Dave Mackay
2. Ipswich Town
3. Sweden
4. Uruguay
5. Black and white
6. So that it would be first in the League alphabetically

QUIZ 392
1. John McGovern
2. Birmingham
3. Poland
4. Hoddle (England), Ardiles (Argentina) and Archibald (Scotland)
5. Colorado, USA
6. Dave Bennett, then with Manchester City

QUIZ 393
1. Dennis Mortimer
2. Duncan McKenzie
3. Feyenoord
4. Brian Marwood, Alan Smith and Michael Thomas
5. Sky blue, navy and white
6. Chris Woods for Nottingham Forest

QUIZ 394
1. Roy McFarland
2. West Germany
3. Johnny Rep
4. Bobby Robson
5. A church
6. Tony Book and Dave Mackay

QUIZ 395
1. Glyn Pardoe
2. Ian Edwards
3. Van der Kerkhof
4. Alan Mullery
5. Silver grey
6. Bath

QUIZ 396
1. Manchester City
2. Gordon Chisholm
3. Stuttgart Kickers
4. Peru
5. Maine Road
6. Clive Allen

QUIZ 397
1. Wolves
2. Kerry Dixon
3. Dino Zoff
4. Kuwait
5. Turf Moor, Burnley
6. Bob Stokoe

QUIZ 398
1. Graeme Souness
2. England
3. AC Milan
4. Ray Clemence
5. Orange
6. £60

QUIZ 399
1. Tommy Smith
2. David Mills
3. Karl-Heinz Rummenigge
4. Zambia
5. Richard Attenborough
6. The term originated from an annual match played in the town of Derby between two local parishes

QUIZ 400
1. Bill Shankly
2. Aston Villa
3. Portugal
4. Denmark
5. They refunded stakes to anyone who had bet on a 1-1 draw (Argentina actually won the match 2-1!)
6. The FA Cup semi-final with Spurs which Watford lost 4-1

QUIZ 401

1. Chelsea
2. Duncan Edwards
3. Goalkeeper
4. Uruguay
5. Twelve
6. Manchester United

QUIZ 402

1. Luton Town
2. Peter Osgood
3. Belgium
4. Marco van Basten
5. Terry Butcher's
6. Queen's Park Rangers'

QUIZ 403

1. Birmingham City
2. Portsmouth
3. Czechoslovakia
4. England
5. Liverpool
6. Lose a match

QUIZ 404

1. Reading
2. Peter Shilton
3. Allan Simonsen
4. 0-0
5. Tom Jones
6. A shot which swerves in the air, its flight path making the shape of a banana

QUIZ 405

1. Manchester United
2. Liverpool
3. Ferenc Puskas
4. Jimmy Rimmer
5. Graeme Souness
6. A drop-ball

QUIZ 406

1. George Best
2. Arsenal
3. Because Eintracht play in Frankfurt, West Germany while Vorwaerts come from Frankfurt-ander-Oder in East Germany
4. Paul Power
5. Anfield, Liverpool
6. West Ham, in 1975

QUIZ 407

1. Everton
2. Millwall
3. Barcelona

4. Italy
5. St Mirren
6. Mike Smith

QUIZ 408

1. Kenny Dalglish
2. Ray Houghton
3. Standard Liege
4. David Harvey
5. Six of their players wore jerseys with the sponsor's name missing
6. Gerry Francis

QUIZ 409

1. Alfie Conn
2. Derek Dougan
3. FC Bruges
4. Eire, in 1949
5. Des O'Connor
6. The Freight Rover Trophy

QUIZ 410

1. Ray Clemence
2. Ron Greenwood
3. FC Porto
4. Roger Milla
5. 'Good Old Arsenal'
6. Keith Hackett

QUIZ 411

1. Newcastle
2. Jimmy Greaves
3. The European Cup-Winners Cup
4. Erwin and Ronald Koeman
5. Burslem, Stoke-on-Trent
6. Stanley Matthews

QUIZ 412

1. Southampton
2. Les Sealey
3. Real Madrid
4. Leopoldo Luque
5. The Nolans (he married Anne)
6. Lincoln City

QUIZ 413

1. Rangers
2. Bob Paisley
3. Lokomotiv Leipzig
4. Costa Rica
5. Claret and amber
6. No

QUIZ 414

1. John Aldridge, Tony Cottee and Alan Smith
2. Nayim

3. Portugal's
4. East Germany (*Deutsche Demokratische Republik*)
5. Barnsley
6. They have all won the European Cup-Winners Cup

QUIZ 415

1. Torquay and Bolton
2. Mixu Paatelainen of Dundee United, who netted for Finland in the 2-2 draw at Swansea
3. Allofs
4. El Salvador
5. Tottenham
6. Telford and Macclesfield

QUIZ 416

1. Joe Harper
2. Leeds United
3. Real Madrid
4. Munich
5. The Baseball Ground
6. Four

QUIZ 417

1. Everton
2. Trevor Christie
3. Jean-Marie Pfaff
4. Roberto Boninsegna
5. Real Madrid
6. It is a team of football experts, employed by the pools companies to give their impression of how postponed matches would have finished

QUIZ 418

1. Ipswich Town
2. Frank McGarvey
3. No
4. West Germany
5. Jimmy Hill
6. Iceland

QUIZ 419

1. Hamilton Accies
2. Derby County
3. Law, Charlton and Best
4. Peter Bonetti
5. Lawrie McMenemy
6. They each scored a hat-trick

QUIZ 420

1. Gordon Lee
2. Paul Hegarty
3. Napoli

4. Switzerland
5. Mick Channon
6. The Drybrough Cup

QUIZ 421

1. Willie McFaul at Newcastle
2. West Bromwich, Manchester City, Norwich
3. Martin Jol
4. Colin Bell and Francis Lee
5. Gary Stevens (the Spurs version, who replaced his namesake, then with Everton)
6. Bobby Charlton

QUIZ 422

1. Jim McLean of Dundee United
2. Middlesbrough
3. PSV Eindhoven
4. Chile
5. Lee Chapman
6. Wycombe

QUIZ 423

1. Rangers
2. Paul Miller
3. Pierre Littbarski
4. Blue
5. He is a supporter of Coventry City who won the FA Cup that day
6. Wimbledon

QUIZ 424

1. Joe Fagan
2. David Langan
3. Manny Kaltz
4. Score a goal in the World Cup
5. Tommy Docherty
6. Terry Venables

QUIZ 425

1. Albion Rovers
2. David Rocastle
3. Inter-Milan
4. Uruguay, Italy, West Germany and Argentina
5. Shinguards
6. Ipswich Town

QUIZ 426

1. Sutton United
2. Robert Fleck
3. Barcelona and Borussia Moenchengladbach
4. Burruchaga
5. Blue and yellow
6. The FA Vase

QUIZ 427
1. Manchester City
2. Paul Madeley
3. Paulo Futre
4. Mario Zagalo (Brazil)
5. Black and white
6. 14, by Liverpool in 1965-66

QUIZ 428
1. Wolves
2. John Robertson
3. FC Mechelen
4. Brazil, in 1970
5. Tottenham
6. He is the physiotherapist

QUIZ 429
1. Terry Cooper
2. David Phillips
3. Barcelona
4. 'The Socceroos'
5. Torquay United's
6. Tommy Smith

QUIZ 430
1. Manchester City and Aston Villa
2. Stan Mortensen
3. It signifies that they are the reigning national champions
4. Graeme Souness
5. Tommy Cannon
6. Colin Harvey

QUIZ 431
1. Alex Ferguson
2. West Ham
3. Poland
4. Oleg Kuznetsov
5. The running of an old people's home
6. Wolves

QUIZ 432
1. Rochdale
2. Michael Robinson
3. Benfica
4. Ian Callaghan
5. Bill Shankly's
6. No

QUIZ 433
1. Ron Saunders
2. Chris Turner
3. Francois Van der Elst
4. 1983, against Northern Ireland in Belfast
5. Everton

6. Players could only be off-side within 18 yards of their opponents' goal-line

QUIZ 434
1. Ally McCoist
2. Frank Worthington
3. Andoni Goicoechea
4. France
5. Newcastle
6. It indicates that any player outside is the required distance from the penalty spot at a penalty kick

QUIZ 435
1. Ray Harford
2. John Bailey
3. It is played over two legs, on a home-and-away basis
4. Neil Webb
5. Manchester City
6. They were all goalkeepers

QUIZ 436
1. Five
2. Ken McNaught
3. Marco van Basten's
4. Mexico
5. Wolves
6. Clyde

QUIZ 437
1. The Scottish First Division
2. Neil McNab
3. Werder Bremen
4. Eire and Northern Ireland
5. They have all scored from long kick-outs
6. Leicester City

QUIZ 438
1. Nottingham Forest in 1978
2. John Hurst – the rest were goal-keepers
3. Gaetano Scirea
4. Austria and West Germany
5. Bristol Rovers
6. Allan Brown

QUIZ 439
1. The FA Cup Final
2. Gary Megson, now with Manchester City
3. Switzerland
4. Gary Mackay
5. 'This is Anfield'
6. No

QUIZ 440

1. Everton
2. John Aldridge
3. Poland
4. Leighton James
5. Aberdeen and Dundee United
6. They have all been manager of Derby County

QUIZ 441

1. Bolton Wanderers
2. Kingsley Black
3. Mancini and Vialli
4. Walter Winterbottom
5. He defected!
6. John Barnes

QUIZ 442

1. They were relegated
2. Arsenal
3. Sammy Lee
4. Yes, against Eire in 1976
5. Three days
6. Andy Gray

QUIZ 443

1. Yes, Queen's Park did in 1884 and 1885
2. Malcolm Macdonald and Alan Hudson
3. Hugo Sanchez
4. Bobby Charlton
5. Ajax
6. Malcolm Macdonald

QUIZ 444

1. Gary Mabbutt
2. Mel
3. Leverkusen
4. Scotland (an own goal in the 1-1 draw with Iran)
5. Leyton Orient
6. Terry Butcher and Chris Woods

QUIZ 445

1. Everton and Sheffield Wednesday
2. Tony Brown
3. Dino Zoff of Italy
4. Terry Venables
5. A car-park for spectators at the adjacent cricket ground
6. Ten

QUIZ 446

1. Brian Clough
2. Allen McKnight
3. Ian Rush
4. Maurice Johnston
5. Stirling Albion
6. The club was formed by the ground staff of the huge Crystal Palace building which housed the Great Exhibition of 1851

QUIZ 447

1. Nigel Winterburn
2. Pat Nevin
3. Harald Schumacher
4. Denmark
5. Halifax Town
6. Chile

QUIZ 448

1. Joe Royle
2. Steve Sims
3. Michael Rummenigge
4. West Germany and Italy
5. Blue
6. Venezuela

QUIZ 449

1. Wilf McGuinness
2. Mark Dennis
3. AC Milan
4. Sweden
5. He said that it 'wasn't one of his best'!
6. Four

QUIZ 450

1. Lawrie Sanchez
2. Derby County
3. Paris St Germain
4. Sweden
5. West Ham
6. CONCACAF

QUIZ 451

1. Arnold Muhren, in 1983
2. The Republic of Ireland
3. Real Mallorca
4. No
5. Partick Thistle and Meadowbank Thistle
6. It is the date of the annual transfer deadline. Players signed after this date are ineligible to play in matches involving promotion or relegation

QUIZ 452

1. Steve Foster, then of Brighton
2. John Burridge

3. Juventus
4. Mick Mills
5. Valley Parade
6. Graham Turner and Billy McNeill

QUIZ 453
1. Phil Thompson
2. Wales
3. Real Madrid
4. Red shirts, green shorts and red socks
5. White City
6. Steve Nicol of Liverpool

QUIZ 454
1. Old Trafford
2. Middlesbrough
3. Rudi Voller
4. 'The Wembley Wizards'
5. Their White Hart Lane ground was unfit for use because of unfinished building work
6. The 1981 UEFA Cup

QUIZ 455
1. Frank McAvennie
2. They all sported a moustache
3. Nick Deacy
4. Maradona
5. Leicester City
6. Smith – Alex, Jim and Denis respectively

QUIZ 456
1. The Mercantile Credit Centenary Trophy Final
2. John Robertson
3. Sampdoria
4. Harold Shepherdson
5. A Dukla Prague away strip
6. John Hollins

QUIZ 457
1. Manchester United, in 1965
2. Alan Mullery
3. Ivan Golac
4. The Soviet Union (it's Russian for USSR)
5. Everpool
6. Barclays 'Young Eagle'

QUIZ 458
1. Wolves
2. Rangers
3. Mats Magnusson
4. Brazil
5. 'Good Morning Mexico'
6. Derry City

QUIZ 459
1. Old Trafford, where Chelsea beat Leeds in the 1970 replay
2. Leeds United
3. UEFA decided that artificial pitches (such as QPR then had) were not to be used in European competitions
4. Tostao
5. 'The Railwaymen'
6. Mark Lawrenson

QUIZ 460
1. Peter Shreeves
2. Steve McMahon
3. The captain
4. Cameroons
5. Ray Wilson
6. Paul Merson

QUIZ 461
1. Newport County
2. Joe Mercer
3. Hamburg
4. Yugoslavia
5. Davie Cooper
6. David Speedie (for Chelsea v Manchester City in the Full Members Cup Final)

QUIZ 462
1. Tottenham, in 1961
2. Fulham
3. Atletico Madrid
4. Jimmy Greaves
5. Nelson Mandela
6. Partick Thistle

QUIZ 463
1. St Johnstone
2. Birmingham City
3. Dinamo Bucharest
4. Scotland and Northern Ireland
5. Martin Peters
6. Swansea

QUIZ 464
1. Chelsea
2. Crewe Alexandra
3. Bordeaux
4. Uruguay
5. Shrewsbury Town
6. Maidstone United

QUIZ 465
1. Mel Machin
2. Wales
3. Robert Prytz
4. Preben Elkjaer
5. Darlington
6. The Football League

QUIZ 466
1. Ipswich
2. Steve Sutton
3. Italy
4. East Germany
5. Kenny Dalglish
6. St Mirren

QUIZ 467
1. Aberdeen, in 1984
2. Alex James
3. Jose Antonio Camacho
4. Nanninga
5. He scored a hat-trick
6. Tommy Hutchison

QUIZ 468
1. Bradford City
2. David Pizanti
3. Alessandro Altobelli
4. England
5. Charlie Nicholas
6. Steve Perryman

QUIZ 469
1. Burnley
2. Dave Beasant
3. Orgryte
4. Colombia
5. Steve Foster
6. Celtic, who beat Liverpool on penalties

QUIZ 470
1. Leeds United
2. Steve Bull
3. Switzerland's
4. Brazil
5. Grimsby Town
6. Yes, Clapton Orient played two games there in 1930

QUIZ 471
1. The FA Charity Shield
2. Alan Sunderland
3. Steaua Bucharest
4. Canada
5. Aberdeen
6. John Bond

QUIZ 472
1. Arthur Rowley, with 434 in all
2. Scotland
3. AC Milan
4. Emlyn Hughes (62 in all)
5. They each have two Football League clubs
6. Richard Gough of Rangers

QUIZ 473
1. Watford
2. Willie Johnston
3. Nottingham Forest
4. George Best
5. It was a 'rap'
6. Lincoln City

QUIZ 474
1. West Ham and Bristol City
2. England
3. Dynamo Dresden
4. Eusebio
5. Johnny Giles
6. Egypt

QUIZ 475
1. Brain McClair
2. Roy Aitken
3. Hamburg
4. Terry Butcher
5. St Johnstone
6. Jimmy Hill

QUIZ 476
1. Tranmere Rovers
2. Kevin Ratcliffe
3. Marseille
4. Valencia
5. George Best
6. Dundee United

QUIZ 477
1. Kenny Sansom
2. Mark Hateley
3. Jupp Derwall
4. Tony Woodcock
5. They built the first cantilever stand with an unrestricted view of the pitch
6. Joe Worrall

QUIZ 478
1. Everton
2. Sheffield United
3. Ajax Amsterdam
4. Bryan Robson and Tony Adams

5. Kenny Dalglish
6. Gordon McQueen

QUIZ 479
1. Lawrie McMenemy
2. Bryan Gunn of Norwich
3. Bob Paisley in 1977
4. Brazilian
5. Millwall's (Jimmy Carter)
6. Steve Harrison

QUIZ 480
1. Garry Parker, Lee Chapman and Tony Cottee
2. Alan Smith
3. Because all matches are played in the same venue – the National Stadium in Ta'Qali
4. No.10
5. It was the first colour broadcast of the match
6. Chelsea

QUIZ 481
1. Gillingham
2. Vinny Jones
3. Jean Tigana
4. No
5. Rugby League
6. Charlton

QUIZ 482
1. They all finished bottom of their respective divisions
2. Norwich
3. Cologne
4. Joe Jordan
5. Tony Galvin
6. Scarborough, Wigan and Maidstone

QUIZ 483
1. Bobby Gould
2. Northampton Town
3. Dasayev and Zubizarreta
4. 1982
5. They came in a mini-bus!
6. Seven

QUIZ 484
1. Jimmy Greaves
2. Mike Galloway
3. Ally McCoist
4. Yellow
5. Bristol Rovers
6. All styles of ball

QUIZ 485
1. Pat Nevin
2. Chris Morris and Mel Sterland
3. Juventus
4. Gullit and van Basten
5. Ossie Ardiles ('Ossie's Dream')
6. Liverpool had previously never lost a match in which Ian Rush had scored

QUIZ 486
1. Brian Stein
2. Burnley and Everton
3. Scotland
4. Spain
5. 'The Seasiders'
6. Bobby Campbell

QUIZ 487
1. Birmingham, Walsall and Shrewsbury
2. Trevor Hockey
3. Eric Gerets
4. Stuart Pearce
5. Peter Beardsley
6. Aston Villa

QUIZ 488
1. Peter Nicholas'
2. Stoke City
3. Italy
4. Both Northern Ireland and Wales
5. Gary Newbon
6. They were drawn away in every round

QUIZ 489
1. Bobby Gould
2. Hull City
3. Uli and Dieter
4. Joe Craig (He came on as a substitute and scored with a header on his first touch)
5. Coventry City
6. Manager Brian Clough

QUIZ 490
1. Peter Shilton
2. Ian Durrant
3. Raymond Kopa
4. Ray Houghton
5. JVC
6. Luton Town, who had been snowbound

QUIZ 491

1. The FA Cup
2. Bernie Slaven
3. AEK Athens
4. The Soviet Union, who won 2-0
5. White
6. Chris Woods and Graham Roberts (who twice had to deputize for Woods during matches)

QUIZ 492

1. Seven
2. Martin Allen
3. Glenn Hoddle and Mark Hateley
4. Alan Ball
5. Kenny Sansom
6. Graham Turner

QUIZ 493

1. Linfield
2. John Stiles, son of Nobby
3. Barcelona
4. Romario
5. Meadowbank Thistle
6. The Beazer Homes (Southern) League

QUIZ 494

1. Andy Dibble
2. Chris Nicholl
3. Frank Rijkaard
4. Gary Pallister
5. They had broken UEFA regulations by allowing action replays to be shown on electronic screens during a European Cup tie
6. Tottenham Hotspur (after 'Harry Hotspur')

QUIZ 495

1. Darlington
2. Frank McLintock
3. Icelandic
4. Uruguay
5. Third Lanark
6. Huddersfield Town

QUIZ 496

1. Liverpool
2. Andy Jones
3. Leo Beenhakker
4. Luxembourg
5. They come down an escalator
6. This is left to the discretion of the referee

QUIZ 497

1. Wolverhampton Wanderers in 1958-59
2. Aberdeen
3. FC Mechelen
4. Chris Waddle and Steve Bull
5. Solvite. Eagle Express became the new sponsors
6. Yes, if they are on the goal-line, e.g. at an indirect free-kick in the penalty area

QUIZ 498

1. John Docherty
2. David Seaman
3. Enzo Francescoli
4. Terry Yorath
5. Hummel
6. Because they had also been relegated to Division Three in 1988 and so were ineligible since the tournament is only for First and Second Division clubs

QUIZ 499

1. Nottingham Forest and Sheffield Wednesday
2. 40
3. Benfica
4. Zaire, 1974
5. Graeme Souness
6. Don Howe

QUIZ 500

1. Bruce Rioch
2. Frank Stapleton
3. Celtic (1967) and Ajax (1972)
4. Under-23 internationals
5. Scunthorpe United
6. 3-0 to the Football League